FIND YOUR FIT

**UNLOCK GOD'S UNIQUE DESIGN FOR YOUR
TALENTS, SPIRITUAL GIFTS, AND PERSONALITY**

JANE KISE, KEVIN JOHNSON, and KAREN EILERS

BETHANYHOUSE
a division of Baker Publishing Group
Minneapolis, Minnesota

© 1998, 2018 by Kevin Johnson, Jane Kise, David Stark, Sandra K. Hirsh, and Karen Eilers

Published by Bethany House Publishers
11400 Hampshire Avenue South
Bloomington, Minnesota 55438
www.bethanyhouse.com

Bethany House Publishers is a division of
Baker Publishing Group, Grand Rapids, Michigan

Printed in the United States of America

ISBN 978-0-7642-3135-3

Library of Congress Cataloging-in-Publication Control Number: 2018957430

Cover design by Dan Pitts
Illustrations by Simon Clare

18 19 20 21 22 23 24   7 6 5 4 3 2 1

Contents

Intro

Make Your Parents Read This!

To the Parents of *Find Your Fit* Readers

In addition to Jane and Kevin's experience coaching adults in career transition and Kevin's background as a pastor to large crowds of students, we're both parents. And Karen has counseled with countless families as their children finish high school. We've navigated the "give them roots and give them wings" process of choosing colleges, discerning majors, and diving into the job market.

We're convinced that all parents want the best for their children. As you walk alongside your teenager, helping them discern the best choices, please keep one thing in mind:

> There is an ongoing, unresolvable tension between finding meaningful work and the realities of the marketplace.

Perhaps you've heard teens say something like, "I can't handle a desk job—I need to be part of something fulfilling, something that I'm passionate about." And they're right. Research bears out that workers who use their inborn skills in service to a purpose they believe in are the most productive workers in America. However, we've heard parents panic when those inborn skills are associated with lower-paying jobs or uncertain career paths. Here are some real-life examples we've encountered:

- ▶ "Our daughter wants to join her friends at an out-of-state college when the one nearest us has a nationally acclaimed business school. Shouldn't she do the practical thing?"
- ▶ "Our son's such a dreamer—he wants to be the next J. J. Abrams. How do we get him to be realistic?"
- ▶ "For three generations everyone in our family has gone to college—and now this child just wants to build houses. Shouldn't we at least make him get a business degree?"

The parental warning to concentrate on marketplace realities may sound loud and clear. Perhaps you're even contemplating tying college funding to "guaranteed" choices such as accountancy, information technology, or medicine.

That's fine, *if* your child's natural design makes those careers suitable. If not, know that many of those who attend *LifeKeys* workshops, the adult version of *Find Your Fit*, are adults who are dissatisfied with their first careers. They overfocused on marketplace realities and wound up miserable, working in environments that don't suit them and that don't match how God gifted them.

Your Teen through God's Eyes

Find Your Fit is designed to help teens see themselves through God's eyes, maybe for the first time in their lives.

Not how they look through the eyes of a media-crazed world that tells them, "It's how you look and shoot hoops that determines what you're worth."

Not how they look through the eyes of school systems that tell them, "It's how you do on standardized tests that determines what you're worth."

Not how they look through the eyes of peers who tell them, "It's whether you're in the right crowd that determines what you're worth."

What teens and young adults discover in *Find Your Fit* about their value and giftedness applies both to what they might do as workers for God's kingdom and to their own career plans—which for many people are one and the same! Through the five lenses we present, teens can explore their God-given design and understand that they are valuable to God. They'll identify their

- interests—and begin to pattern a life of motivation and significance;
- abilities—and realize that they have *many*, even if theirs aren't the ones the world celebrates;
- spiritual gifts—and recognize that God gifts people to work together for purposes bigger than themselves;
- personality type—and understand their natural preferences for working and communicating;
- values—and build a structure for making good, godly decisions.

Why so many lenses? Because so many people find it difficult to believe that they're custom designed for a life of meaning and purpose. We've taken people from age fifteen to ninety through *LifeKeys*. At various points in the process, people arrive at self-acceptance. If someone says, "Even if God did give me these abilities, they aren't worth much," perhaps as she discovers her personality type she'll exclaim, "So that's why I'm different—and I'm still normal!" Only with this kind of self-acceptance are people free to carry out the purposes God intends for them.

Entwined with the process of using our gifts for God's purposes is making career choices—and *Find Your Fit* applies to both. You can use *Find Your Fit* with your teen to help explore schooling options or the world of work.

There are no guarantees for job success these days. Even more important, we all have different definitions of success. If you truly want to help your teenagers get on the right career road—as well as a lifetime of fulfilling service to God—you can help them discover their giftedness by giving them three of the most generous, loving presents you've ever provided.

Your First Gift—Find Your Own Fit

Go through these exercises yourself (or use the adult version, *LifeKeys*). Even if you love your job or volunteer activities, finding your own fit will let you and your teen talk through many issues using the same vocabulary. Look at each other's abilities. In these last years together before your teen leaves home, make the most of your similarities and use your differences to talk through life choices. Odds are good that you have different personality types. Use that information to discover how differently you approach making decisions or using your strengths.

Above all, if your teen's career ideas strike you as impractical or misguided, listen in silence until you have time to review your teen's "All about Me" summary at the end of the book. What within your teen's unique makeup leads him or her to these ideas? Are there ways the idea truly fits your teen? Maybe it *is* a crazy idea—or maybe the two of you are just very different. *Find Your Fit* provides a structure for working through conflicts using facts instead of opinions and emotions.

Your Second Gift—Let Your Teenager Explore

As much as you probably want your teenager to focus on a career so he or she chooses the right technical training or college—especially anytime you contemplate that tuition price tag—too much focus too soon can block the possibility of ever finding an optimal career choice.

More than half the students who start college this year won't finish in five years. One major reason is midstream changes. Students often start with an unresearched, pragmatic career choice. By their third semester of college, many discover they have neither aptitude nor interest to pursue that choice. One of our friends was already accepted into dental school before he spent a single day observing in a dentist's office. He hated it. There he was, his senior year, without any career goals.

The goal of *Find Your Fit* is as much to *broaden* thinking about possible careers as it is to *point toward* possible fields. Your child probably knows what you do. Help your teenager explore a variety of options, especially those far removed from your own experiences. Keep in mind that your teen's ideas are still forming. At that age, they often have only vague ideas about career options or majors, and they often need to feel that they have your permission to explore them. As he or she completes *Find Your Fit*, list different occupations for firsthand research before choosing a technical school or college. Your teen will probably need your help making those connections and finding relevant information.

Your Third Gift—Let Your Teenager Dream

Some surveys show that more than 25 percent of college students are business majors—yet won't necessarily have enough business skills to land a first job. That explains why a third of all pizza-delivery drivers in some areas have a college degree. As school enrollments and job markets fluctuate, it's often the case that more people are training as doctors and lawyers than there are positions in the medical and legal fields. What "makes sense" and seems "a sure bet to getting a job" just may not work.

If your teen's career dreams seem just that to you—impossible dreams—help shape a contingency plan. Maybe your son *will* dance with the Joffrey Ballet, but you might encourage him to get a teaching certificate in physical education. Maybe your daughter *will* be an astronaut, but logging hours toward her commercial pilot's license could be the ticket toward full employment. Help your teen discover an excellent second best they can live with, or another idea that will incorporate some of what they want but in a slightly different direction. The same person who's drawn to being a surgeon might enjoy being a medical laboratory scientist once they know about that option.

Talk about the realistic odds of achieving their ultimate career ambitions, but let your teen decide whether to keep on or change directions. We counsel all too many fifty-year-olds who are still mourning their dream of making their livings as fishing guides or Broadway singers or politicians. In most cases, someone else stomped on their dream. They never had the chance to let it go of their own accord.

Ultimately, one crucial takeaway for your student is to move through a process of informed decision-making. Most teens have never made a truly big decision before, and they often react by freezing up or getting overwhelmed when you try to get them to look at options for colleges, career fields, etc. Sometimes they just need to hear from you that it's okay—that there's a process you'll help them work through. *Find Your Fit* can help jump-start their sense of confidence that they know who they are and what they want, so they can feel empowered to make decisions for themselves.

We hope that *Find Your Fit* will foster meaningful and productive conversations between you and your teenager as well as impart knowledge that helps your teen take the place God designed just for him or her in the work of the kingdom. While we won't guarantee this book will usher in a lifetime of wealth or security, we do believe that working to discover how God made us wisely and values us highly can bring the abundant life Jesus promised.

1

How to Find a Life

Everyone knows someone like Sam. "In high school I was the average kid," he says. Sam could usually outrun his opponents on the soccer field, but he was never the star. He played sax in the school band and taught himself guitar, but he knotted up playing in public. He took plenty of honors courses, but he didn't get straight As.

"I was the class clown," he says. "I made other people laugh, and that got their attention off me and onto the funny things I was saying. The problem is, once you start being funny, you have to keep it up." Even though Sam was involved at school and in church and had some friends, "I always felt like I was on the outside of the inner circle. I didn't feel like I had a place where I belonged."

Then there was Chris, a soccer friend. Chris was always the one who invited Sam to the cool parties, and he seemed totally unbothered by what anyone thought of him. "I wanted to be Chris," Sam says. "I wanted his confidence and that sense of security. He knew who he was and what he had to offer. I was always afraid of not fitting in."

Glance around your immediate world—your school or friend group. What do you see? That guy who is brilliant at math. Or the girl who always finishes a test first. The person with an amazing voice, and another who's the president of every group.

Now look in the mirror. What do you see?

Outside and Inside

Your years in high school and soon after are when most people begin to discover what they're really good at. Ironically, it's also when people worry most about how they rank against everyone else. Battling for a spot in the hierarchy can be exhausting. Some teenagers try hard to rack up achievements to outscore their classmates. Others get discouraged and give up on competing altogether. Almost no one feels like they're winning.

In fact, comparisons are almost always a lose-lose game. The more you compare, the more you feel *less*—less talented, less attractive, less . . . you fill in the blank. Relying on comparisons for how you see yourself isn't helpful. In fact, it can give you the completely wrong idea.

So how do you get the right view of you?

How about this. Instead of looking *outside* at the people you know and the standards you feel you have to live up to, start looking *inside* at the way you're made. And spend some time with the God who made you, who understands you *inside and out*, and no matter what you think, made you on purpose.

Find Your Fit is built on the belief that God made you uniquely and values you highly. While people around you might make you feel as if you have to compete or conform, God has better plans for you. In God's plan, it's more than okay to be exactly who you are.

The Purpose of *Find Your Fit*

Here's the thing. As a teenager or young adult, you're in a time of intense development of your *identity*—your sense of who you are. Along with all your peers, you're attempting to find your thing, your niche, the place you fit. But at some point, almost everybody feels lost! We wrote *Find Your Fit* to equip you for that path of discovery. We want you to understand how normal it is to be unsure about who you are and what you want to do. We want to give you a few crucial tools to understand how God specifically crafted you to be effective in the world.

All three authors of this book have abundant experience working with people making big life decisions. Jane is an expert coach who helps others make the most of their uniqueness in every part of life, from school to work to their most important relationships. Kevin has invested his life as a youth worker, teaching pastor, and career coach. Karen has counseled thousands of young people trying to figure themselves out so they can make smart career and college decisions. Our mission is to give you the benefit of the experience of countless people who have walked this road ahead of you and to give you new perspective to help you find your way.

You're expected to conform in so many areas of life that it may not be obvious to you how God made you uniquely or how that uniqueness should affect the life you lead. To *find your fit* takes effort. Exploration. Discernment. This book helps you do that work. It gives you tools to discover how God has gifted you in ways you've never thought of—and it tells how you can use those gifts to pursue God's best for your life. It will help you know yourself better and prime your thoughts about careers. It can lead you into areas where you can serve God and people. It will encourage you to try new things and spot special interests. Most of all, it will help you find freedom to be what God made you to be.

Finding Your Sweet Spot

When we talk with students about their plans, we're constantly reminded of how big a decision it is to choose a path in life—and how little information most students get to help them find their way. It's like stepping out on the hike of a lifetime without the gear you need to enjoy the adventure.

Can we be honest? Most adults aren't really sure how to help you. They're often only familiar with their own story, and many don't know all that much about other options. The good news is that this book is here to fill you in and help you move forward. There are concrete things you can do to figure things out, and the journey starts by looking inside and understanding yourself better.

As you go through this book, we'll guide you step by step to find out all about you. We'll help you look inside at how God made you. You'll discover five crucial aspects of yourself: your interests, your abilities, your spiritual gifts, your values, and your personality. We'll spend a chapter on each of these five areas so you can get new ideas about you and what you want to do.

This book isn't about us *telling* you what to think, but about you *discovering* what's already there. We'll give you a vocabulary for the unique aspects that make you who you are. You'll confirm things you already know about yourself—and find some surprises along the way.

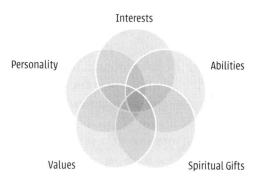

The graphic above, called a Venn diagram, illustrates all five aspects we'll talk about. These noteworthy things about you are all separate, but they also overlap and work together. For example, if you're naturally good at math, you might find that you have a logical personality that values problem-solving. Or maybe you're interested in graphic design and have natural creative abilities that make you effective in communicating a concept.

Everyone has their own unique pattern of who they are, and our goal is to help you notice these various aspects of yourself so you can start seeing how they add up. Wherever they all overlap is a place you want to be—your sweet spot for work, school, or service.

1. **Interests** are the topics, actions, problems, ideas, or trends that attract your attention and draw you in. As you engage with them, they keep you energized and make you want to come back for more. What kinds of things do you do just because you like them? Or just because you want to know more about them?

2. **Abilities** are natural talents you possess. These things come easily to you, whether they're simple or complex, in school or elsewhere. What have you done that you get compliments about? What have you succeeded at that seems to come easy?

3. **Spiritual gifts** are abilities that come to us from God through the work of the Holy Spirit. We don't choose them. God picks them for us and empowers us to impact our world. When has God used you to make a difference in someone's life? What ministry tasks have you seen people do that seem like something you could try?

4. **Values** are the principles and priorities that guide you, especially when you have a decision to make. They're your gut-level rankings of what's important. They influence your choices, and they nudge you toward your best options. What things matter so much to you that you take a stand to defend them? What principles guide you when you make tough choices?

5. **Personality** sums up who you are as a person. These built-in tendencies for doing life include how you get energized, how you take in information, how you make decisions, and how you use your time. What significant traits capture who you are? What's unique about the way you do life?

Every experience you've ever had gives you clues about these things. Think back—what's one thing you tried as a kid but then rejected because it wasn't fun or you weren't good at it? Soccer? Drawing? Piano lessons? Everyone has some of these—things that weren't *your* thing. And you stopped doing them because they didn't fit you, or they didn't fit well with all aspects of you.

As you wind your way through middle school, high school, and college or whatever comes after, the list of things that you have weeded out will continue to get longer, and your focus on what you will pursue will get narrower. That's normal! Over time, all of us get better at seeing what fits us best—the things in our sweet spot. That's what the center of that Venn diagram represents. It's the range of things you could do that incorporate all the best parts of you and put them to use.

Since that's already happening for you, use this opportunity to wrap your head around some new information about yourself. See what you want to weed out and what you want to keep pursuing. (By the way, it's always easier to know what you *don't* want than what you *do*.) The more attention you pay to these things now, the more confident you'll feel as you make decisions for the future.

A Major Decision

By the way, when most people your age think about the future, they think about it like THE FUTURE (cue the flashing lasers, stage fog, and ear-crushing band). It's big and scary and difficult to take in, but simultaneously kind of exciting. Does that sum it up for you?

If you're a student or young adult, chances are you still have decisions to make to answer the pressing question of "What am I going to do with my life?" Decision-making is both nerve-racking and exhilarating. In the midst of all that, how can you work toward smart decisions? And how do you know you're doing what God wants you to do?

Here's one general principle to follow: When in doubt, get more information. (That's what Karen's dad always said, and it works!) A big part of feeling unsure about your future is not knowing enough about your options. For every crucial decision of life, you need to look around and gather information about your possible choices—for example, the majors, colleges, or career fields you're considering. The world won't just hand you this info. You need to get it for yourself.

Never underestimate the power of a little research. It could make a small difference—like between being a geneticist or a genetic counselor. Or it could make a much bigger difference—like between being a nurse or a teacher. One student Karen worked with planned to be an engineer until his research turned up the idea of industrial design. It was a significantly better fit for his creative mind, and that tweak changed not only his major but his whole list of colleges to apply to.

In our experience, the best decisions come from looking *inside* at who you are and what you prefer—as well as what's *outside*, considering and learning more about the options out there for you. For people who want to include God in their decision-making, there's one more element that carries a lot of weight: God's will. Or should we say GOD'S WILL, because it's such a big deal!

What Does God Have to Do with It?

There's a lot that could be said on this topic, but a few important principles will do for now.

1. **God gives you some clear boundaries.** The Bible makes some dos and don'ts plenty clear. Like the walls of a bumper-car rink, these clear commands set obvious boundaries of wrong and right—like "Don't lie," "Don't kill," "Don't steal." Or, as Jesus said, "Love God completely" and "Love others as much as you love yourself." Decision-making within God's will means staying within the walls, making choices that are obvious yeses.

2. **God gives you some freedom to choose.** While God gives us clear direction on moral choices, you also have huge amounts of freedom to choose on other things. Within that bumper-car rink, you have room to zoom around. No Bible verse lists your name and tells you that your life will be best spent as a geologist or by teaching third-grade Sunday school. No Scripture tells you if, where, or when to attend college or what job to take when you finish. Even so, God hasn't left you to spin circles in the bumper-car rink of life.

3. **God built you for a purpose.** We believe that one of the best ways to steer within God's boundaries is clueing in to what God wants you to do by looking at *how you are made*. Look at the rest of God's creation: Eagles soar. Dolphins leap. Cheetahs run. They do what they were meant to do, and they don't try to be anything else. God made you with a unique combination of gifts to fulfill a unique role in the universe. There's peace in that, and we want that peace for you. Paying attention to how God made you guides you into what to do and how to do it.

What Does God Have to Say about It?

If your first job is to learn and stay inside the clear boundaries God announced in the Bible, we believe your second job is to learn to function in creation as you. But there's more to the story about how you and God, together, work out this thing called life. Let's nail down three foundational truths about how God interacts with you.

1. First, remember that God made you and has known you every second of your life, including what will happen every second that hasn't happened yet! Psalm 139:15–16 tells us,

My frame was not hidden from you when I was made in the secret place, when I was woven together in the depths of the earth. Your eyes saw my unformed body; all the days ordained for me were written in your book before one of them came to be.

And, responding to that truth, in verse 14 the psalmist says,

I praise you because I am fearfully and wonderfully made; your works are wonderful. I know that full well.

This passage is one of the most familiar among Christians for a good reason. It reminds us that no matter what we think of ourselves, God knows us intimately and made us on purpose. And even beyond that, we're made well! God's work in us is wonderful, which originally meant "full of wonder." Speaking as career counselors, we can tell you that it fills us with wonder when we see someone starting to grasp that being who they are is *valuable*, that they are needed in the world *just as they are*.

2. On top of that, another essential biblical truth is that God cares about what you're doing in the world, and even has some specific tasks for you to carry out. Ephesians 2:10 (AMP) says something profound:

For we are His workmanship [His own master work, a work of art], created in Christ Jesus [reborn from above—spiritually transformed, renewed, ready to be used] for good works, which God prepared [for us] beforehand [taking paths which He set], so that we would walk in them [living the good life which He prearranged and made ready for us].

The Amplified version of the Bible really unpacks all the meaning of the original Greek that this verse was written in. Read it over a few times until the full truth of it sinks in. Not only did God make you on purpose, but God has gone before you to lay out "good works"—which basically means good things worth doing—for you to accomplish. Does that get you a little more excited about what's coming up in your life? Hope so.

3. The final piece of biblical truth to make sure you hear as we begin is this, from John 15:16:

> You did not choose me, but I chose you and appointed you so that you might go and bear fruit—fruit that will last—and so that whatever you ask in my name the Father will give you.

Just for fun, let's see the Amplified version of this verse, too:

> You have not chosen Me, but I have chosen you and I have appointed and placed and purposefully planted you, so that you would go and bear fruit and keep on bearing, and that your fruit will remain and be lasting, so that whatever you ask of the Father in My name [as My representative] He may give to you.

God has appointed you to go and bear fruit—to be a servant of God who is equipped with both inborn abilities as well as spiritual gifts, making you doubly empowered to do things in this world. God has had bold deeds in mind for you since before the beginning of time and will help you with them. And that work can be fruitful—that is, effective and successful and meaningful! How does that sound to you?

With that profound knowledge of God's love and purpose for you, we encourage you to use this opportunity to climb out of your current day-to-day mindset and begin exploring how God made you and what some of your gifts and "fruit" could be. Don't feel this like a big weight of pressure—we know you might be tempted to—but instead feel it like a tremendous gift. This will happen by the mighty power of the Holy Spirit working inside you. You don't have to figure it all out yourself.

Remember, when God gives you a gift, it's unlike any other. God wired you, knows you inside and out. God is in charge of the universe but isn't an autocrat. The Bible makes this promise to those willing to follow God:

> "For I know the plans I have for you," declares the Lord, "plans to prosper you and not to harm you, plans to give you hope and a future."
>
> Jeremiah 29:11

When God shows you what to do, it's the absolute best for you.

So What's the Catch?

The tools are here. We're giving you a variety of ways to understand yourself, the purposes for your life, and the gifts God chose for you from a stockpile of ultimate wisdom and ultimate love. So what would keep you from finding your fit? *You.* Here's why:

- ▶ You might feel *rushed*: "Who has time for that?" You may feel pushed to just make a decision—to pick a path that everyone says is a sure bet for success. But you have a lifetime of choices ahead of you. Don't join the millions of people punching a clock who didn't take the time to find the right thing, short-changing their own development and their happiness.
- ▶ You might feel *spiritual*: "God says I'm supposed to 'lose my-self'—I just want to focus on Jesus." Look at this process as a way to figure out what you and you alone have to offer to Jesus. For example, Kevin admits to not exploring all of his options as a high schooler because of a warped view that full-time vocational ministry was the only worthy choice for a follower of Jesus. He still found where he functions best, but that doesn't always happen. Part of focusing on Jesus is listening to *all* that God says about you.
- ▶ You might feel *insecure*: "I don't have any special gifts. What if I don't like what I find?" Maybe you play the bassoon better

than anyone else in your school—because no one else plays it. It's an unusual talent, but don't knock it. It got one friend of ours a full-ride scholarship to a top university, followed by a full-time job in a symphony. If you feel like what you have isn't anything great, you may not be fully appreciating it yet!

▸ You might feel *scared*: "I'm not sure I'm any good at anything." If you want to be yourself, you first have to know yourself. Amy Van Dyken—the first U.S. woman to win four gold medals at one Olympics—was a wretched swimmer early in high school. But she persevered. She eventually combined her natural talent, coaches' directions, and a desire to go for gold. Have the courage to identify what you're good at and go for it.

▸ You might feel *smug*: "I don't need to think about this. I've already got it figured out." You may think you already have your life planned out. But chances are good you made those plans without knowing all of what this book will reveal. You can ignore how you're wired. But don't be surprised if someday you've become just another person who did the first thing that occurred to them and had to change direction later.

The catch in *Find Your Fit* is that *you* have to do the work, though we do promise you'll have fun doing it. After all, you're the only person who lives inside your skin twenty-four hours a day. You're the only one with years of experience being you.

So if you're ready, plunge ahead. Take the exercises seriously. Try hard to hear God's heart of love for you in what we say. And go ahead and unwrap God's gifts to you.

2

Making Your Life Matter

Interests

Have you ever gone on an epic road trip—a family vacation, a visit to a distant relative, carpooling with teammates to a faraway tournament, maybe a cross-country drive to Disney World? Whenever you embark on a long drive, the person at the wheel needs to give serious attention to the gas gauge. If you've ever run on fumes and ended up stranded on the side of the road, you know why.

It's stressful to suddenly notice the arrow pointing to a big E, as in EMPTY. Yet when there's plenty of gas in the tank, you cruise on with no worries, confident you can get where you're going.

Maybe you've felt your own personal gas gauge point to E. You need to get something done, but you can't muster the energy. We've all been there with class assignments, but what about things you used to enjoy but just don't anymore? When have you run out of energy for a project, a sport, or an activity that's stopped being fun or interesting? For Karen, it meant dropping piano lessons in favor of choir. Kevin ditched his camera for a new love of telescopes, but lately he's added shooting photos back into the mix. Jane had an adult job that took her deep into finance until she woke up to her dissatisfaction and found her way into psychology and writing.

It's normal if you're realizing that some of the interests you've enjoyed in the past won't make the cut as you move into young adulthood. In fact, a ton of students completely overhaul what they're involved in during the time they're in high school and college. Most people just slowly become aware that certain things don't feel like a fit for the long haul, while other options look more promising.

In everyday life, interest shows up as energy. Think about the first time you tried one of your favorite things—picked up a bow, kicked a ball, baked cookies, or popped open a car hood. That moment was a turning point. As you launched into a new activity, you felt energized, and you keep coming back for more. The bigger the boost you feel, the longer you're willing to do it.

Some interests show up early in life and last a long time. Some come and go. When you're looking toward your future, you want to pay special attention to interests that put gas in your tank long-term and propel you far down the road.

Interests and Passions

Interests come in all sizes. Some are big. They make a noticeable impact on your life. Your thoughts and calendar are full of that mesmerizing thing. Karen works with a high school junior, for example, who spends a huge percentage of his week on hockey. And he's been eating and breathing hockey since first grade!

You might have an interest that dominates your life. Or maybe you have some medium-sized interests—things you enjoy that regularly get chunks of your time and effort. You don't want them to take over your life, but you're happy to be involved. And then there are small-sized interests you might overlook, like how often you read articles about a certain topic, discuss the topic with a neighbor, or watch videos about it.

Your biggest and most enduring interests might rise to the level of a passion, a good term to describe something that engages both mind and heart—that is, it grabs your interest *and* generates strong feelings. A passion is so energizing that you commit your life to it. Sometimes it's a cause (think Martin Luther King Jr.) or a position (like President Franklin D. Roosevelt). It could be a person (like your parents pouring themselves into *you!*) or a group of people (like Mother Teresa showing love to the excluded).

Acting "with God"

Passion can be defined as "a powerful emotion. Fervor, ardor, enthusiasm, zeal."

A bit of word-origin trivia: The word *enthusiasm* comes from the Greek phrase *en theos*, which means "with God." So a worthwhile passion could be anything you pursue with God. And flip that around: Anything you pursue with God is truly worthwhile. While you don't get a superhero suit to wear while dashing from good deed to good deed, God's goal for your existence is for you to contribute something worthwhile to this world. Remember? "For we are [God's] workmanship, created in Christ Jesus for good works" (Ephesians 2:10 ESV).

Passion isn't about sitting in church acting holy. It's not the spiritual equivalent of your mother telling you to take out the garbage. It's caring about something bigger than yourself, important to you and important in the grand scheme of things. It's helping people. Losing yourself in God's higher purposes. Choosing not just to make a living but to make a difference in your world. Finding a passion can be as life changing as getting sucked up in a tornado and deposited in the land of Oz. You'll be doing something important and living connected to God.

The enthusiasm of acting with God is a breed of fun that's different from what you might expect. It's more exciting than going on a shopping spree, more lasting than winning a big game, and more satisfying than getting into the college of your choice. When you're following God and going where your interests and passions lead you, you know you're doing something that matters—no matter what it is! And you can know that you'll have God's help to guide you and help you as you go.

Now, you may be in for some bumps. Doing something meaningful doesn't mean it will be easy. You'll probably decide the struggle is worth it, though, because what you're doing is so *satisfying*.

- ► You might get blisters from hauling away storm debris, but the discomfort fades when you hear the thank-yous from people you help.
- ► You might give up a week's paycheck to take time off and help with a medical mission trip, but the rewards are better than money.
- ► You might get strange looks if you change your major from business to linguistics because you decide you want to teach English-language learners, but if God has truly given you that passion, it will be the best change you ever made.

Keep this in mind: Choosing a career can be an opportunity to fully focus on your passions. It's possible to dream about your passions and your career at the same time. Big hint: As you check out career ideas, focus on choosing a job that makes you feel like you're doing something significant—more than just making money. At the least, make sure the role you dream about allows you time to pursue your passions outside of work time.

Millions of adults say, "If I had to do it all over, I'd have chosen a different career—one that gave me more freedom for the activities that really matter to me. I thought I was being practical, but I feel like I missed out on bigger things." If you find a way to blend your work and your passions, you'll be one of the lucky ones who loves work as much as play.

Some teens have already discovered an interest they're passionate about, meaning they're willing to sink time and effort into it— sometimes in a paid position, sometimes on their own. But if you're still discovering what ignites your energy, keep at it. Passions often show up as you gain more experience in life and work. But you have to pay attention!

Your interests create a pattern unique to you, along with those biggest of interests, your passions. They show where you're willing to expend energy, knowing that you get back even more than you give.

As you consider your interests and passions in the coming pages, we hope you'll be surprised—and yet not. You'll be surprised by things you're interested in without realizing it, and not surprised by things you've always known you love. In this chapter we'll help you identify your most important interests and passions. That's a great place to start as you think about where to point your life in the future.

Targeting Your Future

When you think about where your life is headed, picture it as shooting an arrow from a bow. That arrow moves forward along a trajectory that (hopefully) takes it directly toward the target, maybe even hitting the bull's-eye. Your life up until now has already been on a trajectory, but now, maybe for the first time ever, you have a lot more choice about how and where you direct it.

Having that much choice can raise a lot of questions about who you are and what you want, and we hope that *Find Your Fit* will help you make those choices. We want to help you set a trajectory that moves you toward your very own target—the opportunities for work, school, or ministry that will be a great fit for you. Engaging in the tasks you're made to do will help you tap into the interests and passions God has given you, and knowing what's on that target will help you make future plans.

When Karen talks with students about their college and career options, she always starts by asking questions about their interests—the stuff that person really gets into, both in and out of school. Why? Because if something just isn't interesting, it's not "on target" for that person. It's that simple. The more she can dig into that person's interests, the more obvious that target becomes.

Students don't always have a choice about what they study. Their school or program dictates the courses, and teachers or professors determine the content. Some of it's interesting, some not, some in the middle. You might even feel like you've spent your whole life learning material you don't really care about. Now it's time to start focusing on what you *do* care about, and thinking about your interest level in some different subjects can tell you a lot.

School Subject Interest Chart

Take this chance to ponder how much interest you have in various school subjects. NOW WAIT A SECOND. This isn't about how much you liked or disliked a *class* you took or how much you liked or disliked the *teacher*! This is about the *material*. How engaged were you by what you were learning? Can you see yourself wanting to learn more about that *topic*, even if a teacher is tough, dry, or difficult to follow? That's the true test.

Look at each subject below and list the names of any classes you've completed in that subject in the last few years. Add any subjects not on the list at the bottom. If you haven't taken any classes in a subject, leave it blank.

Then think about each subject overall. What's the trend? How much interest have you had across all those classes? Rate your interest level as of right now in the last column.

1 = "I don't ever want to think about that again." Totally uninteresting, boring, de-motivating.

10 = "I think about this a lot, even when I don't have to." It's fascinating, energizing, motivating.

School Subject	Classes You've Taken	Interest Rating (1–10)
math		
English/writing		
science		
history/social studies		
foreign language		
gym/health		
art/music		
psychology/sociology		
business/law		
construction/engineering		

As you scan your chart, what do you see? One or two clear winners? A bunch of high-middling scores—6s and 7s? Maybe everything looks about the same? This is different for every single person, and there are no right or wrong answers. If there's an obvious winner, then your path into the future might be clear. But for most people, a combination of interests shows up in their choices. You could be a researcher who writes, a coach who teaches, or an entrepreneur who uses math!

What we want to get you to think about is this: Where is your energy going? Chances are good that you got a lot more enthusiastic about some subjects than others, and that's where you can start seeing future options that could be on target for you.

Check out the chart below for specific career or major ideas that correspond to your answers above. Circle a few that you might want to follow up on.

If you like . . .	You might want to check out . . .
math	math, physics, computer science, accounting, actuarial science
English/ writing	English, communications, theater, journalism, writing, advertising
science	biology, chemistry, biochemistry, environmental science, physics, premedicine, communication science, food science, geology
history/social studies	history, political science, philosophy, economics, classics, geography
foreign language	Spanish, French, German, Chinese, etc.; international studies, linguistics, international business, anthropology
gym/health	exercise science, athletic training, biology, physical therapy
art/music	music performance, music business, art/music education, graphic design, art, interior design, fashion design, art/music therapy
psychology/ sociology	psychology, sociology, anthropology, criminal justice, education, social work, neuroscience, religion
business/law	business management, accounting, finance, marketing, pre-law, hospitality management, supply-chain management
construction/ engineering	engineering (civil, mechanical, electrical, etc.), drafting, robotics, construction management, information systems, industrial design
other areas	

Seeing some things you want to learn more about? If so, record them here:

_____

_____

_____

Looking at options in school gives you ideas of what might be on target for you. Take this list home and show your parents, or talk to a teacher or guidance counselor at school to learn more about opportunities in these areas. Or check out the Occupational Outlook Handbook online at https://www.bls.gov/ooh. This site has real-world info on all kinds of different career options.

Most people are interested in several things, both in and out of school. If you're afraid that picking a major or career means that you have to shut down all your interests except one—don't worry! Your path through life will often let you combine your interests in new and interesting ways. And you can keep using your interests outside of work as well.

Finding Your Passions

Discovering your passions builds on what you know about your interests. As we've talked with people who've found the things that supercharge their energy, we've learned that they discovered what they care most deeply about in one of four ways. Which sounds most like you?

"Do One Thing Well and Do It Everywhere" people

Whatever these people like to do, they'll do again and again. If they like to grill burgers, they'll grill them at church, at company picnics, at the beach, in a house, with a mouse. If they like to pound nails, they'll build sets for the school play, fix siding for Grandpa, rehab homes for the disadvantaged. They know what they like, and

Making Your Life Matter

they use the same talent or interest in lots of places throughout their lives.

"Be a Joiner" people

Another set of people likes options. They check out what different dreamers are doing and pick a vision they can get passionate about. If they like a friend's idea to fill Easter baskets for kids whose homes were destroyed by a tornado, they'll knock on doors for donations. If they think a homeless shelter or food shelf or free medical clinic serves a great purpose, they'll look for opportunities to join in. Pretty soon they'll be as passionate about the cause as if they dreamed it up themselves.

"It Was There All Along" people

Some people don't have to look far to find something they're passionate about—they just need to look around and notice what they are already devoting their time and energy to. The opportunities are all around. They rake the yard of the elderly woman next door. They train as a peer counselor because they once got so much help from one. Or they help out at home with their own brothers and sisters. They find things to do right under their nose, and they get more into it as they go.

"I Have a Dream" people

Some people find it easy and energizing to dream big—they like thinking about the big world out there and the big things they could do in it, even if they haven't tried those things before. They could be interested in anything, from curing the common cold to helping the homeless to installing new irrigation systems in the Gobi Desert. They don't have a problem finding passions. They just have to narrow them down to what they can do in one lifetime.

Pick Your Passions

So what did you decide? Are you a . . .

- ▸ *"Do One Thing Well and Do It Everywhere" Person*—do you look for chances to use a specific talent, interest, or spiritual gift in a variety of arenas?
- ▸ *"Be a Joiner" Person*—are there certain leaders or ministries who chase visions or missions that appeal to you? Are there roles to fill within those efforts that fit with your gifts?
- ▸ *"It Was There All Along" Person*—if you broaden your definition of passions, might yours appear right where you are, in the settings you sit in all the time?
- ▸ *"I Have a Dream" Person*—do you find it easy and exciting to simply dream about what you might do for God?

Flip first to the description that fits you best and work through those passion ideas first. Don't try to do this all at once—but complete one exercise right now. After that, set *Find Your Fit* aside for a day and give your ideas time to simmer on the back burner of your brain. Then reread what you came up with and try another exercise.

For the "Do One Thing Well and Do It Everywhere" People

1. Think about the talents or interests you're already developing in your life. Which do you most enjoy using? List other ways you could use them.
2. Check out the following list of skills and talents. If you were going to help with a project, which would you prefer to use? Which are fun for you? Can you think of others? Check the ones that sound most like you, and don't think of this list as complete—write down anything else these items make you think of.

- ☐ artistic expression
- ☐ balloon-tying
- ☐ babysitting
- ☐ car repairs
- ☐ carpentry
- ☐ cleaning
- ☐ coaching
- ☐ computers
- ☐ construction
- ☐ cooking
- ☐ counseling
- ☐ crafts
- ☐ dance
- ☐ digging
- ☐ drama
- ☐ driving
- ☐ electronics
- ☐ feeding the hungry
- ☐ financial planning/ budgets
- ☐ foreign languages
- ☐ gardening
- ☐ graphic arts
- ☐ graphic design
- ☐ health clinics
- ☐ home repairs
- ☐ interior design
- ☐ managing people
- ☐ mathematics
- ☐ media
- ☐ mime
- ☐ music— instrumental
- ☐ music—vocal
- ☐ office administration
- ☐ office tasks
- ☐ organizing events/ parties
- ☐ painting
- ☐ photography
- ☐ political pursuits
- ☐ publicity
- ☐ puppets
- ☐ reading
- ☐ remedial tutoring
- ☐ research
- ☐ selling
- ☐ sewing
- ☐ speaking
- ☐ storytelling
- ☐ teaching
- ☐ teaching English as a second language
- ☐ time management
- ☐ word processing
- ☐ working outdoors
- ☐ writing/journalism
- ☐ _____
- ☐ _____
- ☐ _____
- ☐ _____
- ☐ _____
- ☐ _____

For the "Be a Joiner" People

1. Find out what ministries and missions your church supports. Look at your school. Ask your parents. Which strike you as important? What kind of help do they need? How might you fit into their activities or plans?

_____

_____

_____

_____

2. For more places to get involved in your wider community, check volunteermatch.org or other volunteer portals in your part of the world.

_____

_____

_____

_____

3. List where you've volunteered in the past. What did you do? Would you do it again? What gifts and talents did you use?

At school:

_____

_____

In your family:

_____

_____

At your church:

_____

_____

Through civic or student groups like Scouts:

_____

_____

For the "It Was There All Along" People

1. List all of the roles you play. Are you a student? Neighbor? Someone's child? Someone's sibling? A patient? A customer? An

employee? A friend? What problems do you notice right around you? What could you do about them?

_____

_____

_____

_____

_____

_____

_____

_____

2. You might like holding babies. Or maybe you don't want to be near kids until they're old enough to play chess. Some people are fascinated by hospital environments. Others shriek when they see blood. Look through these groups or situations. Who do you wish you could help? Do you have personal experience or lots of contact with friends or relatives that are part of these groups? Some of these ideas may appeal to you now—or later as career areas.

Age groups

☐ babies
☐ teens
☐ toddlers and preschoolers
☐ college/young adults
☐ early elementary school
☐ singles
☐ late elementary school
☐ young marrieds
☐ all children
☐ parents
☐ peers (your own age or grade)
☐ senior citizens

People with practical needs

☐ education (or tutoring)
☐ housing needs
☐ finance/budget issues
☐ legal advice/concerns
☐ healthcare assistance
☐ maintenance or repair needs

- ☐ parenting concerns
- ☐ peer counseling/mediation
- ☐ prayer ministries
- ☐ workplace issues

People with counseling needs

- ☐ substance abuse
- ☐ marital counseling
- ☐ grief support
- ☐ families not getting along
- ☐ support groups
- ☐ spiritual direction/discipleship

Ministries to specific populations

- ☐ refugees
- ☐ ethnic minorities
- ☐ the poor
- ☐ neighbors/community
- ☐ the disabled
- ☐ people who are ill
- ☐ church visitors
- ☐ new kids at school
- ☐ younger students
- ☐ students who need to improve study skills
- ☐ business and professional men/women
- ☐ international students
- ☐ missionaries
- ☐ the unemployed

For the "I Have a Dream" People

1. If you had no fear of failure and limitless time and resources at your disposal, what would you do (besides winning the lottery and traveling around the world)? What is your dream for your future?

2. Name some people who have accomplished something that you would like to do or who have had a tremendous positive impact on your life. Because of them, what causes or purposes might you want to focus on?

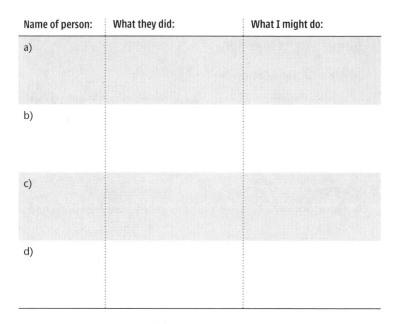

Name of person:	What they did:	What I might do:
a)		
b)		
c)		
d)		

After completing two or three of these exercises, take a moment to record some of your clearest interests on page 235, "All about Me." Then talk over what you're figuring out with someone who knows you well—a friend, parent, group leader, coach—and see what they have to say. One thing about our interests and passions— they're almost always contagious! Share your ideas and see who might be inspired by your idea and want to help.

Where to Go from Here?

1. **If you just don't seem to be passionate about any-thing, relax.** For some people, identifying things they want to do takes years. But look again at the interests you already have. Which ones might cause you to join in enthusiastically— with what God is doing? What wrongs in the world make you mad enough to take action? Do you value yourself enough to think that God can use you?

2. **Read the paper, watch the news.** What would you change if you could? Which news stories grab at your heartstrings? Think about these things in terms of passions and careers. What could you pursue?

3. **Try out different ways of serving people firsthand.** What's rewarding about it? What's hard? Which do you do best?

4. **Think about *why* you do *what* you do.** It's the key to making things you love to do match the things you do with God. When you act with God, you look beyond *what* you're doing to *why* you're doing it and *who* you do it for.

   Have you heard about the two stonecutters? When asked what they were doing, one said, "I'm cutting stones." The other said, "I'm building a cathedral."

   Or the two insurance agents. One said, "I work so I can make my house payment." The other said, "I work to make sure that if a parent dies, the family isn't left penniless as I was as a child."

5. **Ask your parents, teachers, and other adult friends the big "What if?" question.** What if they could rechoose their career? What would they do differently?

Push Back Those Doubts

As you reflect on all that God might be stirring up in your mind or heart, all kinds of doubts or fears might pop up. God hands out all kinds of interests and passions, and they might seem big, small, near, far, practical, or crazy. You can trust God to unfold your life step by step and to put the next thing to do in front of you. But you might make three huge mistakes as you try to figure out what God designed you to do.

1. **You can't wait around until you're absolutely certain you know what God wants you to do.** For one, your interests are an expression of *you*. God designed you to dream

about what might make the world a better place. To be bold. You don't need a thunderbolt from heaven to go ahead and act. For two, it's hard for God to steer you if you're sitting still. If you don't do anything, you'll never know that you have gas in the tank and the motor is running. Instead of being stuck, assume that if you're somehow using your abilities or spiritual gifts—and what you do seems to make God real to others—then you're acting wisely. You can't be far from what God has in mind for you.

2. **You can't excuse yourself from stepping out just because you aren't the next Billy Graham.** God needs Joan of Arcs and Abraham Lincolns. But for every person who helps multitudes, God needs thousands more who can hold hands and hear and help problems one-on-one. And God doesn't seem to clone the big-time players—God designed Lincoln and Rosa Parks and Billy Graham for their own places, times, and purposes—and you're designed for yours.

3. **You can't plan everything in advance.** Jesus once talked about a man attacked on his way to the city of Jericho. As the man lay beaten and bleeding on the road, two holy men walked by. Each looked at the man and said, "Not my job." The third man who came along found all sorts of ways to help—even though he was a foreigner, an enemy of the beaten-up guy. That "Good Samaritan" didn't worry if wiping up blood and hauling a man to safety was one of his gifts. If you're "on the road to Jericho" and run across an emergency of any kind, *do what it takes even if it isn't your gift or passion.* Chuck everything you learned about yourself in *Find Your Fit* to meet that big-time need, because God is putting it right in front of you.

Now and Later

Remember, no matter who you are, you have a lifelong call to do good things in the world, and that journey is going to unfold over time. If it's too much to think about your whole life right now, you might want to think about interests *now*, in the short term, and passions *later*, what you might do with your future. Maybe all you have time for right now is trying to make it to track practice—that's okay. But you won't be ready for the next season of your life if you don't think about what it might be.

So if you're drawn to something that is too big for you to handle right now, think about what you might do to get ready for it.

- ▶ If you want to be a missionary, start by exploring another language.
- ▶ If you want to serve God by being an at-home parent, help out by watching little kids.
- ▶ If you want to serve God by changing the system, study politics. Intern with a social worker. Or at a law office. Or with an environmental agency.
- ▶ If you want to serve God as a doctor, lawyer, teacher, pilot, anything, talk to people who do that and consider what God might want you to do in that position.

Jesus taught again and again on being ready. "Be dressed for action and have your lamps lit; be like those who are waiting for their master to return from the wedding banquet, so that they may open the door for him as soon as he comes and knocks" (Luke 12:35–36 NRSV). Now's your chance to get ready for a future of enthusiasm with God, to seize the moment, to prepare now to join God at work.

Locating Your Life

Abilities

I f you're a wolf, how you spend your life all depends on where you're born. Minnesota wolves hang out in the forest and eat deer, while Alaska wolves live on the tundra and dine on mice. No choice in your occupation. Or diet. All wolves run, jump, track, and bite, some just a bit better than others. Wolves don't pause to ponder how happy they are about their fate. They just *do*—driven by instinct, corralled by environment.

But you're a *homo sapiens*. You have choices.

Unlike wolves, humans have different abilities. You were born with a big bunch already built into you by God. Besides that, your environment is constantly expanding. Your whole world is changing, churning out new ideas and new opportunities by the microsecond. On top of that, *you* are growing. Each day—if you spend it well—gives you new skills, new wisdom, new resources to follow God into new things.

You can do the human equivalent of moving north and eating mice, or heading south and dining on deer. Your world gives you a chance to choose—different places to live and work, different people to hang out with. Distinctly diverse futures.

Smiley Faces and Last Picks

Problem is, by the time you graduated from elementary school, you probably stuck yourself with one of three labels:

- *"I've got this."* You know you're smart, athletic, attractive. You make friends easily. You got a string of smiley faces on your papers in kindergarten, and since then you've assumed there's little you can't do.
- *"I lost out."* Somehow you've gotten the message that life isn't kind. Maybe you draw art that even your mother doesn't love. Maybe you struggle at school, or maybe you've been the last person chosen for every team you've ever been on.
- *"I don't want to think about it."* Some days are good, some not so great. You feel average. You have no grand dreams and no major phobias, so you brush off how you might fit into the future.

Any of these ways of looking at yourself—blowing up or blowing off your abilities or ignoring them altogether—misses the truth about you. Thinking you can be anything you want—that's a fantasy. Feeling you're as worthwhile to the world as a clump of sod—that's a dirty lie. Indefinitely delaying thinking about you—that's just not a good idea because you'll waste your life and miss out on all the fun.

Parents carry pictures of their kids on their phones. You carry a picture of yourself in your brain. Unfortunately, whatever picture you carry—can we be blunt?—you don't see yourself with total accuracy. You don't see yourself the way God sees you. And as you pegged yourself as good-at-everything, bad-to-the-bone, or forever-stuck-in-the-middle, you were probably missing one crucial piece of information: *God made you with a purpose in mind.* Look again at what Ephesians 2:10 (NRSV) says about why God made you:

> For we are what [God] has made us, created in Christ Jesus for good works, which God prepared beforehand to be our way of life.

God designed you to do good stuff. To accomplish something. And God has given you the ability it takes.

You Deserve a Break Today

Do you doubt that God could have fantastically good plans for you?

It all hangs on whether you recognize the gifts God has built into you.

You'll have a hard time seeing your own gifts if you're blinded by the blaze of highly visible abilities. People cheer for Olympic medalists, big moneymakers, and Nobel Prize winners. And that's likely to make you think whatever gifts *you* have aren't any big deal. Face it: If you aren't a superstar of some sort at a young age, it might not seem obvious to you or anyone else that you're talented.

Talents are more than being able to survive a piano recital without your fingers tying up in knots or being able to lick the tip of your nose with your tongue. They're broader than that. The abilities we're talking about are so big you can think of them as gifts, a wild variety of things you can be good at. God's interest isn't limited to people who can wow a crowd. Despite the way some abilities dazzle, the world really doesn't revolve around viral personalities. Whatever abilities you have, they're part of God's design to keep this planet spinning. They aren't second best.

Sure, you can practice a lot and get better at lots of things—but many of those are really *skills*, not *abilities*. What's the difference? An ability is something you can do already that practice takes from good to great. Maybe Mom put your cat drawings on the fridge when you were a preschooler, but she asked you to start designing the family Christmas cards once you'd taken an art class. If you also love to draw, that's an ability. If drawing lessons teach you the basics but sitting down with a sketch pad still doesn't thrill you, that's a skill.

Think about some of your everyday actions—abilities, really—that could bring applause from God:

- Do friends come to you with their problems? If they know you'll listen well, that's an ability. Not everyone knows how to hear people.
- Can you rescue a teacher when the latest classroom technology dies? Not everyone has technical prowess.
- Is your bedroom a model of tidyness? Not everyone has a knack for organization.

You might have dozens of gifts like these—abilities that won't get you an appearance on late-night television but which will let you take your place in God's show. So how could you have missed them?

Warning: Hidden Treasures Ahead

Abilities can stay buried for a long time because you don't look for them. Or you downplay them. Or you don't recognize them as gifts.

There's another huge reason you might not have found your unique abilities until now. You might have gone along with the crowd and picked ho-hum classes that don't let you explore, push you to excel, or give you an opportunity to discover out-of-the-ordinary fields.

Or think about how you spend your free time—lessons, hobbies, sports, extracurricular activities. How did you choose those? By what your friends did? By picking from what was offered after school or at a nearby park? Because your mom or dad prodded you? Chances are you saw only a few possibilities compared with all that is out there.

Once you hit college or tech school, though, your choices expand exponentially. Sure, there's likely a set of core courses to knock off, but you also get a huge smorgasbord of schedules and teachers and subjects.

And in the world of work, your choices explode. There are thousands of jobs you don't even know exist. To top it all off, there are truly significant things you can do that you might not get paid for. Not to mention new areas to search out and stuff to do just for fun. If you're going to be smart in how you choose between all these options, you've got to understand how you're wired.

Decoding Your Brain

Price scanners decode what look like random lines to pull up all sorts of information about a product. You may feel as indecipherable as those stripes of black and white. Believe it or don't, however, there *is* order in how you're put together. And the right type of decoder can tell you a lot about you.

For decades, people have used a theory of "interest areas" in the world of work* to find their fit. Why? Work is where you spend a major portion of your life. (More on that later.) But it also clues you in to your abilities, because people tend to seek work that they're hardwired to do well. Accountants tend to do well with math, counselors are good listeners, and so on. These work-based interest areas are a crucial description of what you like, what you are like, and what you do well.

Psychologists and others who study abilities have noticed that people and their abilities tend to cluster in six areas and have similar themes that run through their careers. They're grouped because they relish *similar tasks*—they like to do the same things. They enjoy *similar co-workers*—they share common interests with the people they work with. They're attracted to *similar work environments*—they like to work in groups or alone, in settings structured or loose, noisy or

*John Holland's theory of vocational choices is the foundation for this section. His work was the basis for the Strong Interest Inventory, available through your school counseling center or local community college if you want to dig deeper.

quiet. And they share similar abilities—people choose careers that let them shine. Here is a list of the six themes:

- ► Realistic [R]
- ► Investigative [I]
- ► Artistic [A]
- ► Social [S]
- ► Enterprising [E]
- ► Conventional [C]

Think of the world of work as a hexagon. You can use it to find the "pieces" where you'll best fit in:

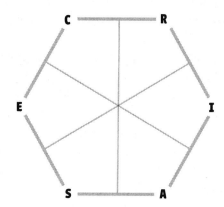

The themes closest to each other have the most in common—R and I, for example, are more similar than R and A. It's likely you have more than one theme that appeals to you. Most people identify with a blend of at least two or three, generally ones that are close to each other. Having a blend of opposites, like R and S, is normal, too, just not as common.

Use the next pages to find out which themes best describe you, and then we'll go on to finding your specific abilities. We start each page with a basic description of each type, then roll out a variety of characteristics that help differentiate types. See where you spot yourself, and then rejoin us on page 78.

Checking out the Themes

1. Flip through the next several pages and just look at the cartoons. Which picture would you like of you in the yearbook? Choose one or two of the cartoons that fit you best and concentrate on those pages first.

2. Pull out a pen or highlighter as you read through the descriptions on the pages you chose first. What sounds like you? Have you tried any of the things described? Ignore what you "should" be. What are you really like? If you're truly stuck, ask a parent, teacher, or other adult who knows you well. Do they see patterns in what you choose to do with your time?

3. When you've finished reading the descriptions for the themes you chose first, go back through and read the others, again highlighting anything that sounds like you. Once you've read through all of the descriptions, rate each theme on how well it describes you: (1 = This describes me well; 2 = Parts of the description sound like me; 3 = This isn't me at all)

___ Realistic

___ Investigative

___ Artistic

___ Social

___ Enterprising

___ Conventional

Not to keep any secrets, Jane is SAI and Kevin is IAS—both are writers (A) who like to help people (S) but spend hours with our heads in books and other research (I). Karen is SAE—her ability with people (S) and creative problem-solving (A) mix with leadership and business know-how (E).

4. Now you can use these themes to guide you in finding your abilities. Turn first to the pages that describe your top theme. Some big tips: Don't worry what your friends will think. Forget about being modest. Read the description of each ability and ask yourself, *Is this something I like to do? Would this be fun to try if I get the chance?* Then decide whether it is one of your abilities. Give each a score from 0 to 10:

   0 = Never done and don't want to

   5 = I'd like to try this *or* I've enjoyed this and think I could do it well with more experience

   10 = I could do this all the time and love it!

   You probably won't have all the abilities in your top theme, but chances are you'll have several of them.

5. If you come across an ability you've never tried—like performing in a play or operating heavy machinery—think of how you've seen others using that gift. Can you picture yourself doing similar things? Does it strike you as something that would be easy or hard to learn?

6. Do the same for all of the themes—read through the ability descriptions and decide which ones you have. You may have at least one in each of the themes, even those that don't sound much like you. For example, Jane chokes on most Conventional tasks, but she does have an ability for managing time and priorities.

7. Once you've searched for your abilities in all six themes, go back through and highlight your top five to ten abilities, the ones you *know* are yours. The ones you most like to use. Write those on page 235, "All about Me."

8. If you can't come up with at least five, sit down with an adult who knows you well and go through this process again. What do they see in you? What might they suggest you try so you can discover the abilities you haven't noticed yet? They're there. Remember, God designed you with a purpose in mind.

If you're a Realistic type, chances are you grew up wanting to be outside at every chance—running, climbing, jumping, enjoying nature. Your favorite toys might have included building blocks, trucks out in the sandbox, or "real" toys like workbenches, ironing boards, and lawn mowers. You may also enjoy athletics or dance—anything that requires coordination.

In school, Realistics prefer hands-on activities—constructing models rather than just reading about different habitats, for example. You do best when teachers convince you that what you are learning is useful. Realistics might save money toward tools or gear for hobbies, gas and insurance for a car, camping equipment, or fees for lift tickets, fishing licenses, etc.

Realistics . . .

- are DOERS
- ask, "How does it work?"
- work with THINGS

Things Realistics do or dream about trying

- sports
- hunting, fishing, camping
- whitewater rafting, bungee jumping, rock climbing
- training, raising animals

- working with or operating cars, boats, planes, mowers, etc.
- gardening

Realistic heroes

Indiana Jones (adventurer and archaeologist), Rocky (prize-fighter), Amelia Earhart (pilot and explorer), Sally Ride (astronaut), Peyton Manning (football player), Bear Grylls (adventurer)

Realistics get in trouble for . . .

- blowing off homework you don't see as useful in "real life"
- running around when you're supposed to sit still
- taking things apart to figure out how they work

Realistics might like work that . . .

- lets you make a tangible difference you can touch or see
- uses large or fine motor skills
- allows for pragmatic approaches to problems
- lets you focus on things rather than on people, ideas, or data

Typical Realistic careers

engineer, forester, driver, building contractor, police officer, pilot, military officer, athletic trainer, industrial arts teacher, animal trainer, environmental scientist

Realistics might volunteer to . . .

paint houses, shovel snow, provide transportation, refinish/repair furniture or machinery, lead outdoor activities, provide food or supplies

Realistics would rather . . .	Others might see Realistics as . . .
► be part of the stage crew than perform ► solve a problem alone than with a group ► go bowling than go to an art museum ► share your life savings than your feelings	► reliable, cool in a crisis ► apt to take physical risks ► hating to be the center of attention ► wanting to take action, not sit around talking

Realistic Interests and Abilities

If this is one of your top themes, chances are you have some of these abilities. If you've never done it—like putting out a forest fire or operating machinery—think of times you've seen others using that talent. Can you picture yourself doing similar things? Does it strike you as something that would be easy or hard for you to learn?

Realistic Abilities	When have I used this? Is it fun for me? Does it feel natural? Was it easy to learn?	SCORE: 1 = hate it 10 = love it
Mechanical aptitude Knowing how things work, understanding and applying the principles of mechanics and physics		
Operating equipment/ driving/piloting Handy at running pieces of equipment or driving vehicles		
Manual dexterity Skilled at using hands or fine tools in woodworking, sewing, cooking, etc.		

Realistic Abilities	When have I used this? Is it fun for me? Does it feel natural? Was it easy to learn?	SCORE: 1 = hate it 10 = love it
Building mechanical or structural devices Capable with designing, assembling, or fixing things		
Physical coordination Able to get muscles moving in the same direction; has the agility needed in sports, skilled trades, etc.		
Organizing supplies or spaces Able to sort and store things effectively, making finding and maintaining materials easy		
Taking physical risks Attracted to activities or occupations that can be physically dangerous		
Emotional stability and reliability Able to react calmly to situations and stay on course		

If you're an Investigative type, you probably asked "Why?" dozens of times each day growing up, if you didn't have your nose in a book. You might have collected and classified shells, insects, or rocks or simply spent time observing ants or clouds—analyzing to figure out how nature operates. Maybe you loved games, puzzles, or video games that challenged your mind.

In school, Investigatives often prefer science or math classes. You may research topics on your own that you're curious about, or get involved in activities like a quiz bowl team or robotics club. Investigatives might use their money to buy things for complex hobbies like astronomy, sailing, or rock climbing. You might also spend it to upgrade your computer or phone or to invest in books.

Investigatives . . .

► are THINKERS

► ask, "Why is it that way?"

► work with THINGS and IDEAS

Things Investigatives do or dream about trying

► doing scientific or laboratory work

► programming a computer

► going on an archaeological dig

► researching, theorizing, solving complex problems

- reading scientific, philosophical, and other nonfiction books and magazines
- mastering complex hobbies—skiing, chess, etc.

Investigative heroes

Sherlock Holmes (detective extraordinaire), Woodward and Bernstein (the reporters who broke the Watergate story), Madame Curie and Albert Einstein (revolutionary scientists)

Investigatives get in trouble for . . .

- ignoring any school subject you aren't really interested in so you can spend loads of time on things you like
- reading or being lost in thought instead of paying attention in class
- challenging your parents or teachers when you think they're not being as logical as you

Investigatives might like work that . . .

- lets you handle ideas or data rather than people
- requires many years of education to build expertise
- involves theory or research and allows independence and independent thinking

Typical Investigative careers

chemist, physician, psychologist, science teacher, pharmacist, college professor, inventor, research and development manager, systems analyst, computer scientist

Investigatives might volunteer to . . .

set strategies or long-range plans, research background data, provide computer skills, collect or organize data, design surveys or studies

Investigatives would rather . . .	Others see Investigatives as . . .
▶ design your projects than follow directions ▶ solve a problem alone than with a group ▶ work at a library than at a retail store ▶ study math than give a speech	▶ independent, self-motivated ▶ absorbed by their interests ▶ original and creative ▶ scholarly, intellectual

Investigative Interests and Abilities

If this is one of your top themes, chances are you have some of these abilities. If you've never done it—like inventing a new widget or theorizing where no one's gone before—think of times you've seen others using that talent. Can you picture yourself doing similar things? Does it strike you as something that would be easy or hard for you to learn?

Investigative Abilities	When have I used this? Is it fun for me? Does it feel natural? Was it easy to learn?	SCORE: 1 = hate it 10 = love it
Inventing Able to imagine or produce useful things or theories, especially in technical or scientific areas		
Researching Good at investigating or experimenting to discover information, test theories, or find ways to apply knowledge		

Investigative Abilities	When have I used this? Is it fun for me? Does it feel natural? Was it easy to learn?	SCORE: 1 = hate it 10 = love it
Conceptualizing Can think up and develop abstract ideas or theories		
Working independently Able to work well without guidance or input from others		
Solving complex problems Able to solve difficult situations using logic or data		
Computer aptitude Good at programming or designing systems and software		
Synthesizing information Can pull together information from different sources and make it understandable		
Theorizing Able to cook up explanations, find connections, or project future trends		

If you think back to elementary school, Artistic types probably were labeled as creative, musical, artistic, dramatic—or as day-dreamers. Your favorite toys might have included craft supplies, musical instruments, props for acting, story-books, or anything that lets loose your imagination.

In school, Artistics do best when allowed to color outside the lines and add a fresh touch to assignments. Many like to write and do best when they like a subject and can learn about it their own way. Artistics might use their money to buy tickets to museums, theatres, or for books or art supplies. You might also prefer to dress originally, making a statement through what you wear.

Artistics . . .

- are CREATORS
- ask, "What if I/we did it this way?"
- work with IDEAS

Things Artistics do or dream about trying

- acting or performing musically
- painting, sculpting, photography
- reporting for the school newspaper or radio station
- writing poetry, stories, or novels
- attending dance, theater, or music concerts
- directing videos, plays

Artistic heroes

Ansel Adams (legendary photographer), Jane Austen and William Shakespeare (world-class writers), J. J. Abrams and Steven Spielberg (brilliant directors), Georgia O'Keefe (innovative artist)

Artistics get in trouble for . . .

► daydreaming, having your head in the clouds
► insisting on self-expression and uniqueness, wanting to do things your way
► producing beautiful projects that didn't exactly follow directions

Artistics might like work that . . .

► allows you to work in unstructured environments where you can set your hours
► lets you work alone or with one or two others, with creative control over your projects
► is in less businesslike settings: museums, libraries, education, nonprofits

Typical Artistic careers

advertising executive, attorney, librarian, musician, reporter, broadcaster, minister, photographer, artist, public relations director, graphic designer

Artistics might volunteer to . . .

be on a drama team, share musical or artistic talents, take part in onetime creative efforts, design and make decorations, do publicity

Artistics would rather . . .	Others might see Artistics as . . .
► write a story than a report ► set your own hours than follow a schedule ► go to an art museum than play cards ► take music lessons than organize anything	► creative and imaginative ► nonconformist, free-spirited ► expressive, sensitive ► unstructured, flexible

Artistic Interests and Abilities

If this is one of your top interest themes, chances are you have some of these abilities. If you've never done it—like performing in a play or redesigning your living room—think of times you've seen others using that talent. Can you picture yourself doing similar things? Does it strike you as something that would be easy or hard for you to learn?

Artistic Abilities	When have I used this? Is it fun for me? Does it feel natural? Was it easy to learn?	SCORE: 1 = hate it 10 = love it
Writing and reporting Can communicate clearly through writing, including reports, letters, and publications		
Verbal linguistic skills Adept at learning languages, using and comprehending spoken words		
Musical expression Able to compose music or perform music with voice, body, or instruments		

Artistic Abilities	When have I used this? Is it fun for me? Does it feel natural? Was it easy to learn?	SCORE: 1 = hate it 10 = love it
Acting Can relate emotions or portray a character through performance on stage or film		
Creative problem-solving Able to find unusual solutions to tough issues, especially in artistic forms or in relationships		
Drawing/painting/ sculpture Find ways to use art as a means of expression		
Creative design Able to work with spatial concepts, like in graphics, interior design, or architecture		
Creative use of color Able to coordinate colors and patterns, such as in clothing design, decorating, etc.		

The Social Person

Growing up, Social types are friends with everyone—you have natural people skills. You often liked playing school and house, where you could practice teaching and caring for others. You also like games that allow for socializing and forming groups, especially if everyone can join.

Socials look forward to school because of the friendships you develop. You tend to enjoy group learning activities and working cooperatively. You want to pass on to others what you have learned. You might prefer classes like English and social studies to more scientific subjects. Socials might use their money for extracurricular activities, going out with friends, group service or mission trips, and hobbies that let you be with others.

Socials . . .

- ▶ are HELPERS
- ▶ ask, "How can I/we make a difference?"
- ▶ work with PEOPLE

Things Socials do or dream about trying

- ▶ organizing parties, social events
- ▶ traveling with friends
- ▶ volunteer work, religious activities
- ▶ being a foreign exchange student—or hosting one

- ▶ working with younger children
- ▶ developing and maintaining relationships

Social heroes

Mother Teresa (Catholic nun who served the poor in India), Bono (musician and humanitarian), Oskar Schindler (hid Jews from the Nazis), Martin Luther King Jr. (pastor and civil rights leader), Rachel Carson (environmental crusader)

Socials get in trouble for . . .

- ▶ talking too much, passing notes, and texting in class
- ▶ spending too much time on your phone/social media
- ▶ sticking your nose in other people's business

Socials might like work that . . .

- ▶ allows you to serve others in environments that emphasize cooperation
- ▶ is in organizations that help people (like hospitals, schools, religious organizations, etc.)
- ▶ involves communicating with others—clients, students, patients, or co-workers

Typical Social careers

elementary schoolteacher, social worker, religious professional, parks and recreation coordinator, physical therapist, nurse, counselor, retirement home administrator

Socials might volunteer to . . .

organize fundraisers, provide child care, plan social events, do peer counseling, tutor, lead small groups, provide hospitality

Socials would rather . . .	Others might see Socials as . . .
▶ work with a group than work alone ▶ tutor a younger child than drive a car ▶ help plan a party than work with numbers ▶ make a friend than read a book	▶ friendly and cheerful ▶ concerned for the welfare of others ▶ kind and generous ▶ ready to listen, tactful

Social Interests and Abilities

If this is one of your top themes, chances are you have some of these abilities. If you've never done it—like teaching a class or counseling someone—think of times you've seen others using that talent. Can you picture yourself doing similar things? Does it strike you as something that would be easy or hard for you to learn?

Social Abilities	When have I used this? Is it fun for me? Does it feel natural? Was it easy to learn?	SCORE: 1 = hate it 10 = love it
Teaching Skilled at instructing, demonstrating, training, or guiding others in learning facts or concepts		
Listening and facilitating Able to encourage others to volunteer information and discuss issues or topics, either one-on-one or in groups		
Counseling and understanding Able to give advice and guidance that fits the needs of others		

Social Abilities	When have I used this? Is it fun for me? Does it feel natural? Was it easy to learn?	SCORE: 1 = hate it 10 = love it
Conversing/informing Offering hospitality, talking and listening one-on-one or in small groups about events, issues, or personal concerns		
Being of service Considers how to help others and acts voluntarily		
Evaluating character Can spot the motives and values of other people		
Being empathetic and tactful Good at noticing how others feel and acting accordingly		
Working with others Able to establish good working relationships based on trust and respect		

Once again, think way back to elementary school. Enterprising types were the natural-born leaders, ready to take charge. Your kindergarten teacher may have told your mom that you were "keeping the other kids in line." You may enjoy competitive sports or convincing your brothers and sisters to do your chores for you.

In school, Enterprisers may spend a lot of time figuring out how to get around the rules or get elected class president. If you're on a sports team, it will be a prestigious one and you'd probably like to be captain. You can sell anything from wrapping paper to popcorn and argue effectively with every teacher in the building. Enterprising types might use earnings for the latest and greatest clothes, tickets to the biggest concerts, or any of the finer things in life.

Enterprisers . . .

- ▸ are PERSUADERS
- ▸ ask, "How can I/we succeed?"
- ▸ work with PEOPLE and DATA

Things Enterprisers do or dream about trying

- ▸ being president—preferably of the country
- ▸ partying with the in crowd
- ▸ debating, giving speeches, persuading others

- ► running a business
- ► vacationing at expensive places
- ► belonging to prestigious clubs, fraternities, or sororities

Enterprising heroes

Bill Gates (leader and philanthropist), Bill and Hillary Clinton (quintessential politicians), Mark Cuban (entrepreneur and team owner), Warren Buffett (CEO and investor), Oprah (media mogul)

Enterprisers get in trouble for . . .

- ► getting others to do the work on group projects while you "supervise"
- ► sweet-talking people into doing anything you come up with
- ► finding loopholes or ways around the rules

Enterprisers might like work that . . .

- ► is goal oriented, where you can measure your success
- ► lets you lead your own endeavors and spend at least some time in the limelight
- ► provides a good living or a high salary

Typical Enterprising careers

sales, management, marketing, human resources director, banker, public relations, financial planner, TV announcer, urban planner, politician

Enterprisers might volunteer to . . .

take leadership roles, spearhead promotional efforts, recruit others, give speeches, raise funds

Enterprisers would rather . . .	Others might see Enterprisers as . . .
▸ lead than follow ▸ give a talk than write a report ▸ study politics than study biology ▸ compete and debate than research anything too deeply	▸ ambitious, adventuresome ▸ witty, talkative ▸ optimistic and full of energy ▸ impressed with status and possessions

Enterprising Interests and Abilities

If this is one of your top interest areas, chances are you have some of these abilities. If you've never done it—like risking money in the stock market or giving a big speech—think of times you've seen others using that talent. Can you picture yourself doing similar things? Does it strike you as something that would be easy or hard for you to learn?

Enterprising Abilities	When have I used this? Is it fun for me? Does it feel natural? Was it easy to learn?	SCORE: 1 = hate it 10 = love it
Public speaking Can communicate clearly in front of a live audience		
Selling Able to convince others to purchase products or services		
Persuading Skilled at getting others to accept an idea, value, or point of view		
Leadership Able to get others to work together and direct people's efforts toward common goals		

Enterprising Abilities	When have I used this? Is it fun for me? Does it feel natural? Was it easy to learn?	SCORE: 1 = hate it 10 = love it
Management Can plan, organize, and direct projects and resources to reach goals		
Negotiating Able to help others in listening to the opinions or demands and reach agreement or compromise		
Taking action Able to respond decisively in emergency or stressful situations		
Adventurousness Willing to take above-average financial and interpersonal risks		

The Conventional Person

If you're a Conventional type, you probably seldom got into trouble growing up—you kept your room clean, finished your chores, and never lost the pieces to your games and puzzles. Your favorite toys might have included dolls, blocks, trains, props for playing school, and games with set rules.

In school, Conventionals like subjects where success comes from mastering a set of rules, such as spelling and math, preferring topics with concrete answers to those with heavy use of theory or creativity. Conventionals often enjoy joining Scouts or organizations like sports leagues. You might not spend much money, saving it for a big-ticket item like a first car. You may also be organized about earning money—developing regular customers for lawn mowing or babysitting.

Conventionals . . .

- are ORGANIZERS
- ask, "How can I/we make that happen?"
- work with DATA and THINGS

Things Conventionals do or dream about trying

- collecting anything and everything
- organizing belongings, supplies
- sight-seeing, visiting popular historic or amusement sites
- building models—from rockets to doll houses

- crossword puzzles, structured games
- owning a cabin or vacationing at the same resort each year

Conventional heroes

Queen Elizabeth II (longest serving monarch of England), H&R Block (the people who help the rest of the country file their taxes), Mister Rogers (who always wore the same sweater)

Conventionals (if you get in trouble at all) get in trouble for . . .

- telling on other kids for not following rules, being a tattletale
- pestering teachers, asking too many questions like, "Is this going to be on the test?"
- being stubborn, insisting that you know the right way to do something

Conventionals might like work that . . .

- emphasizes accuracy and care with details
- offers a set schedule where you can predict what your days will be like
- involves organizing and establishing routines or processes

Typical Conventional careers

accountant, banker, office manager, small business owner, business education teacher, production manager, mathematics teacher, professional organizer

Conventionals might volunteer to . . .

keep records, perform office tasks, organize supplies and equipment, establish procedures, do accounting/auditing, supervise volunteers

Conventionals would rather . . .	Others see Conventionals as . . .
▶ be efficient and accurate than be creative ▶ adhere to a schedule than go with the flow ▶ keep club records than start a new club ▶ go to a movie than act in a play	▶ neat, accurate ▶ pragmatic ▶ methodical, organized ▶ contained and contented

Conventional Interests and Abilities

If this is one of your top themes, chances are you have some of these abilities. If you've never done it—like setting a budget or organizing an event—think of times you've seen others using that talent. Can you picture yourself doing similar things? Does it strike you as something that would be easy or hard for you to learn?

Conventional Abilities	When have I used this? Is it fun for me? Does it feel natural? Was it easy to learn?	SCORE: 1 = hate it 10 = love it
Organizing Able to arrange data, money, study schedules, assembly lines, homes, etc., in a structured way		
Evaluating and appraising Able to accurately estimate the value or significance of things: real estate, antiques, investments, businesses, etc.		
Attending to detail Aware of the small pieces that make up the whole, as in printed words, administrative tasks, or the environment		

Conventional Abilities	When have I used this? Is it fun for me? Does it feel natural? Was it easy to learn?	SCORE: 1 = hate it 10 = love it
Managing time and priorities Good at arranging activities and schedules to consistently meet deadlines, goals, and appointments		
Calculating and mathematics Adept at working with numbers and figures— adding, subtracting, multiplying		
Systematizing Able to sort information or things for ease of use		
Persistence Good at follow-through and patience in handling responsibilities		
Stewardship Known for careful and conservative handling of money, data, and resources		

So What Good Are Abilities?

Why is it important to know your abilities?

Knowing your abilities preps you to make the most of your free time. You know about plenty of sports and hobbies. But take a trip to the magazine section of a big bookstore to see how many different ways there are to spend your non-school hours. Awareness of your abilities shows you what you like and why—and identifies related interests you may want to try.

Knowing your abilities clues you in to how God wants to use you in this world. Your abilities hint at where you can serve effectively. Why, for example, do some people live to tell others about their faith in God? We'll see later that there is a *spiritual gift* of evangelism, but evangelists often have Enterprising abilities like public speaking and persuasion. Would you rather be in a drama? You're probably an Artistic. Would you just as soon stay off stage and pass out bulletins and take the offering? You might be a Conventional.

Knowing your abilities helps you like yourself for who you are. Tanner—a Realistic—was a shy, scrawny kid who built in the rafters of his garage the coolest fort in the neighborhood. His power-tool prowess made him a natural to head up set construction for his high school's lavish musicals. That stage crew experience earned him the nickname Stanley—as in the tool company—and led to a job at one of the country's premiere theaters. The knowledge of hydraulics he learned working backstage teamed up with a good education to take him into the medical technology field.

Knowing your abilities can help you find your fit in the world of work. No single test or source of information can scream, "Go be a fireman," or, "You should start your own business," but knowing you're Realistic or Enterprising alerts you to the likelihood that you'd do well in those fields.

Stepping into Your Best-Fit Job

The goal of *Find Your Fit* isn't to push careers or rush you into premature decisions. Our intent is the opposite—to let you explore all your options and understand why you likely would enjoy some jobs more than others.

**Truth #1: Big satisfaction comes from
doing what God made you to do.**

**Truth #2: In the adult world that means
finding a job that fits you.**

Why is sorting out the job thing so important?

In just a few years, you will enter The Working Zone. Of the 168 hours in your week, you will spend

- ▸ 60 hours at work, including commute time (more if you live in a busy city)
- ▸ 54 hours sleeping (6 on weeknights, 12 on the weekend)
- ▸ 21 hours eating (more if you wash dishes)
- ▸ 10 hours cleaning (washing clothes, cars, etc.)
- ▸ 10 hours running errands (buying groceries, calling home, etc.)

That leaves about 13 hours a week to do what you want to do, unless . . . *your work is something you want to do!* If you just "get a job," something that pays the bills and finances a house full of grown-up toys, you have less than two hours of free time a day. If you *want* to go to work, suddenly half of your waking week is fun.

Right now school might feel like a prison. You do your time, but you live for activities and weekends. It would be great to fix that, but it may not be possible—for now, that is.

But consider this: Finding work that's actually fun can happen—and the fun doesn't depend on the size of the paycheck. Look at the adults around you. Which ones can't wait to get back to their desks? And which ones hate Monday mornings? Lots of people hate work—and it's no coincidence that the most heart attacks happen at around 8:00 a.m. on Mondays! But people who like what they do say they find it *interesting*, find meaning in its *bigger purpose*, or find they *do it well*. Really happy people find all three are true. They make a living. Find fulfillment. Better their world. Adult fun is finding work that aligns with the way God made you.

Making Work Your Playground

We aren't cracking the whip to make you responsible. We're telling you that what you do for laughs can be what you do for a living. Sound good?

Exactly what you do with an ability depends on your aptitude (your raw abilities), application (how hard you work to develop that aptitude), and achievement (what you accomplish with those abilities). It depends on how hard you work and on what you decide is important to you.

Moreover, what you want to do has to react with reality. You have to weigh, for example, whether you want to be one of the eight hundred violin majors (no joke!) who vie for each spot in a professional symphony. Things you'd enjoy as a vocation (your means of making a living) may need to become your avocation (a hobby that may or may not make money). You might choose a different venue for your ability. Lots of those violin majors, for example, spice up church services or have great fun teaching kids to play.

There are thousands of careers out there, but there are some fast ways to narrow down your possibilities.

First, let's get rid of what you can't do. You can't be *anything* you want to be. Yes, in many countries you have free access to any career, but if you flunked a physics test because you don't know what a ball bearing is, you can cross engineering off your list. If you're allergic to cats mentally and physically, you're not going to be a veterinarian. And if listening to people's problems annoys you, don't be any kind of counselor.

Second, you can't choose a career just for the money. Or prestige. Or power. When you're twenty and full of energy, you can probably get good enough grades to jump-start a career even if the classwork bores you. But turn the clock ahead twenty years. Now you're middle-aged, probably with a mortgage, family, and loads of grown-up responsibilities you never expected sapping your strength. Try sitting at your desk doing something that makes the dullest subject in school seem incredibly fascinating. Not only that, but chances are that the person in the office next door *loves* the same job and does it at least as well as you without half the effort. Adults have a word for what happens to you as you sit and wonder why work is so hard: burnout.

But you *can* start tuning in to your own design. You can forget what everyone else is doing and take some chances. After all, if you never pick up a power saw, how will you ever find out if you're cut out to work with wood? If you never give classes like English, social studies, or biology an honest chance, how will you ever know you weren't built to excel or at least do well in those areas?

Third, few people just know what they want to be when they're sixteen. The key is finding the *range* of occupations that might fit, not choosing one now only to find out later that you didn't know enough about it. You want to head in the right direction—college, vo-tech, on-the-job training, or a variety of ways to serve your country or community. You want to pick the right type of school—business, service industry, liberal arts, engineering.

Ask your parents and teachers if they are doing what they wanted to be when they were ten or fifteen or even twenty years old. When Jane was a college freshman, twenty-two of the twenty-four women (not Jane) on her dorm floor said, "I'm going to be a doctor," at their first meeting. Guess what? The group produced exactly one MD. Someone who knows from a young age what he or she wants to do for life is the exception, not the rule.

Another example: When Kevin was in junior high and his mom had cancer, he decided he wanted to be a biochemist. He had great biology and chemistry teachers, fed treated sewage to mice and studied the results, and got hired as a lab tech when he was only seventeen. It wasn't until college that he figured out that the precision and repetition of lab work drove him crazy.

And Karen? She got fascinated by politics in high school, majored in political science, and even chased her dream to Washington, DC, for her first job. It wasn't until she worked for a senator for a year that she realized she didn't really fit in with the values and personality of the people around her.

So Where Do You Go from Here?

As busy as you are right now, life only gets more hectic. That means *right now* is your time to explore areas that might interest you. That process of exploration is your best chance to test what you've learned about yourself and your abilities.

1. *Sample classes.* Scope out the subject matter as well as the people who do well in a class—and actually enjoy the studying it takes to do well. If you're still in high school, check out community colleges and organizations for offerings. Be honest about the obvious: Which school classes so far have you liked the most—other than that American history class where you could catch up on sleep or the chemistry class where you had the cute lab partner?

2. *Do different jobs.* If you have any choice about part-time work, go for exposure to different fields before money. In other words, if you can make more money waiting tables than working as an orderly at a nursing home, the real question is this: Would you rather explore the hospitality industry or get a feel for health care professions? It's not all about money. So make part-time jobs count. Don't waste your summers.

3. *Explore things you love.* Someone will end up designing LEGO kits. Someone really will start up the perfect boutique restaurant in

your town. Someone gets to manage major league baseball teams. Check out what it takes, what other careers that might be easier pathways to success are closely related, or ways to build up your abilities until you're a talent to reckon with doing something you love.

3. *Volunteer.* This is a great way to test out whether you really have a certain ability and—great news—churches have very low entry requirements. They'll let you try almost anything at least once. If you can, ask someone you trust to observe you and give honest feedback.

4. *Spend a day with professionals.* Prepare questions beforehand so you know what you want to learn—nothing worse than wasting someone's workday. What did they want to be when they were little? What might you do right now to gain experience? What's the best part of the job? What's the worst part? (By the way, catching your interviewee on a bad day will make any job sound unappealing.)

5. *Explore schools that excel in areas that might interest you.* You may not have the money, grades, or interest to attend top schools, but shoot high. Look at online catalogs and see what the best schools offer so you can tailor your program wherever you go. Whatever kind of training you want to pursue, comparison shop. Visit several schools.

6. *Visit your school counselor.* He or she can provide you with ideas for jobs. What you see now might not be relevant by the time you graduate or hit your twenties and thirties or beyond. Think *fields* that fit your abilities.

7. *Check out online resources.* You might need some M&M's and some patience, but since you can't job shadow for every occupation you might consider, this is a great place to start.

► The powerhouse online site for using this information is https://www.onetonline.org/find/descriptor/browse/Interests/. Search jobs in your top area—Kevin would search Investigative—or use your full combination, like IAS. Click on specific jobs and find out the skills they need. For example, did you know video game designers are English grammar stars? And need to be great listeners? They work indoors every day and say that being great at teamwork is essential. The site has this information for over 900 occupations.

You'll find thousands of jobs described—from cocoa-bean roaster to pediatrician. Check out skills needed—compare to your abilities!—physical demands, years of schooling required. And you can choose an interest category—like craft arts or sports—and see all the jobs listed. (Just an example: Craft arts included engravers, picture framers, fiberglass model makers, sign painters, and a whole lot of others you've never heard of.)

► Another great site houses what used to be a huge library-only book called the Occupational Outlook Handbook. You can now find the data on salaries, job requirements, and trends in hiring and industry health at https://www.bls.gov/ooh/.

8. *Develop some general ideas of what careers fit you—or definitely don't fit you.* Take notes from people already in these jobs of what is essential to them—and use the online resources to go deeper. Examples might be

► *Sales:* You'd better like people—and be able to handle rejection.

► *Financial Brokerage:* You'd better be interested in multiplying money (and cool under pressure when million-dollar deals fall apart).

► *Pilot*: Settle into the calm of a check-and-recheck routine—and ponder if you want to be the first to die in a crash (after all, planes don't back into mountains).

► *Accounting*: You'll love it if you love numbers—and start now saving up sleep for the crazy hours you'll likely work during tax season.

► *Teaching*: You gotta have a love for people—because teaching even at the college level offers surprisingly little time to hole up in the library alone with a stack of books.

9. *Be fearless.* The God who designed you knows how to get you to the finish line. The moral? Instead of paralyzing yourself with the fear that you'll pick the wrong route, start drawing a map. There are lots of possible roads that end up at the same destination—just make sure you get on one that's going in the right direction for *you*.

4

Fitting In with God's Work

Spiritual Gifts

Step into the mind of God for a moment.

You crafted a world full of people, crazy human beings you love so much that you sent your Son to bring your kind reign to earth. Building a spiritual kingdom is a task too big for humans to do on their own, so you dispatch the Holy Spirit to live in each person willing to join your work. Powered by the Spirit, these people act. They bring compassion and love to the world. They encourage others and spread joy. They invite family, friends, and strangers to follow God. They speak truth to rulers and kings.

Those bold deeds are signs of what the Bible calls "spiritual gifts," spiritual abilities that help the world know and follow Jesus.

Many followers of Jesus don't understand these practical tools or know which ones they have. If you ask people to identify their own spiritual gifts, they might name things like friendliness, patience, good health, or a sense of humor—good things, but not what the Bible deems spiritual gifts.

The Bible promises us that once we become part of the body of Christ, we each receive spiritual gifts: "Now to each one the manifestation [revelation, unveiling, evidence, demonstration, gift] of the Spirit is given for the common good" (1 Corinthians 12:7, our amplification).

Spiritual gifts come in a variety of shapes and sizes. God gives us gifts like *encouragement*: comforting others who feel abandoned or hopeless. Or *teaching*: revealing God's Word so that others figure it out. Or *evangelism*: sharing faith in a way people find inviting.

The Bible contains several lists of spiritual gifts—check out 1 Corinthians 12:1–31 and 14:1–30; Romans 12:4–8; and Ephesians 4:11–13. Many Bible students think those long and varied lists might only be samples of ways God gifts people. To keep this introduction to spiritual gifts straightforward, however, we're grouping gifts. To help you understand the main types of gifting without getting bogged down in descriptive detail, we'll look at evangelism, helps, leadership, discernment/prophecy, encouragement/mercy, faith, hospitality, giving, teaching/wisdom/knowledge, and healing/miracles/tongues.

Spiritual gifts help us build God's kingdom of love and fulfill God's plan for the world. If you're a follower of Jesus, you've got 'em. You may have a gift you don't know about. Yet your gifts really exist.

Unwrapping the Gifts

Picture a decked-out Christmas tree with gifts stacked underneath—a tree with one problem: Weeks after Christmas, needles cover the unopened presents.

You'd have to be crazy to leave a pile of Christmas gifts unopened. But that slowness to rip through the wrapping is how too many Christians approach the special abilities we receive to carry out God's purposes.

So why do Christians let gifts rot under the tree, unwrapped and unused? Most likely because we're afraid to look inside. For five reasons:

1. *We don't know spiritual gifts exist.* Maybe they're under a tree in a room we never enter—we think it's so holy it's off limits. God intends people to get going and growing in gifts from their first glimmer of that belief, yet we might figure God waits until we know everything about faith before unleashing gifts on us. Not so.

2. *We fear we'll hate what we receive.* Just like with any of our other interests and gifts, we worry our spiritual gifts will be something less than good. Rest assured, God has better taste in gifts than an aunt who gives ugly sweaters.

3. *We're afraid God will ask us to use our gifts.* Deep down, most of us fear that God will require us to do something we'd rather not do. As if our spiritual gift will arrive with orders to be a missionary and a one-way ticket to Ukarumpa (that's a real place in Papua New Guinea). Or a command to make friends with a sworn enemy. Well, maybe. But that's all up to God, the Gift Giver who knows us better than we know ourselves and who came to give us abundant life.

4. *We may think we're too young.* Tell that to Jesus, who taught in the temple at twelve, or Timothy, who was likely still a teenager when he began partnering with the apostle Paul. God, of course, knows when we're ready for specific assignments, and God stands ready to use willing hearts of any age.

5. *We may be confused by controversy.* Some Christians argue—a lot—about which gifts God gives today. Some feel strongly that God long ago stopped passing out supernatural gifts like healing, miracles, tongues. Those squabbles can scare people off from discovering and using even uncontroversial gifts. *Find Your Fit* talks about possibilities, about the range of gifts you *might* have. Most gifts are no-brainers no one objects to.

Don't sweat it if supernatural gifts do or don't show up in your life. Check at your church and you'll probably hear that most Christians agree that how and where gifts appear is ultimately God's choice. And gifts let us be part of God's plan.

God's Double Dare

Pay attention to two messages here:

First, *dare to believe you have a spiritual gift*. The Bible tells us that "each one" has a gift. Not just well-known leaders. Not just long-winded teachers. Not just the kid who wins the prize for best share at the closing campfire of a church retreat. God doesn't put a warning on the gifts that says, "For use only by professionals. Don't try this at home."

Since you have a spiritual gift, does that mean you're destined—or doomed, depending on how you look at it—to be a pastor or something?

Nope. There's a major difference in where and how Christians use their gifts. Think of this distinction: There are *formal* and *informal* ministries. You can do a formal ministry like teaching Sunday school, or an informal ministry of teaching kids in the neighborhood. You can be part of a formal evangelistic team that tries to tell your town about Jesus, or informally talk to peers at school. Informal doesn't mean less intense. It means less top-down, less organized by an organization or institution. Paid jobs like pastoring are formal ministry. God doesn't call many to that role. Instead, most of us are sent out to be willing workers in the midst of our everyday lives.

Second, *dare to use your gift*. God gives us gifts for "the common good." The goal of gifts isn't to make us feel great or important but to get work done. After all, the task of carrying out God's work hasn't gotten any easier in the last two thousand years. Even though the number of workers has grown from twelve disciples to many millions, the earth's population grew from a couple hundred million to nearly eight billion, and the world doesn't look much like the kind of kingdom God intends. Technology and the illusion of Christian megastars mask how necessary you are to God's plan. God still needs all of us who are willing to use our spiritual gifts.

Spiritual gifts may look a lot like our interests and abilities. The difference isn't always so much in what you do as why you do it.

You can pound nails through a *Realistic* ability to make a living, or you can pound nails using the spiritual gift of *helps* to show God's love by building a house for a needy family. When you actively use your spiritual gifts, you're being God's hands on earth.

You Got the "Right" Gifts, Right?

Go back to Christmas morning. Sure, sometime or another you've gotten a present you didn't need or want. But you could almost always count on people who love you to do their best to bless you with thoughtful gifts within their means. God amps up that love to infinity and has unlimited knowledge and power to give you the right spiritual gifts.

Even in Paul's time, people were jealous of the spiritual gifts of others. They envied leaders, prophets, teachers, and especially those who seemed to have supernatural powers or the ability to speak in tongues, "the languages of angels." Paul tried to show how senseless this is:

> What if your whole body were made up of hands? No feet, no eyes— how would you see or hear? But God didn't do it that way. Instead, we have eyes and feet and hearts and hands, all right where they're supposed to be.
>
> And your eye can't say, "Hand, I don't need you," or, "I'm better than you, liver." No, God designed us so that we need every part of our bodies. We all need to stay part of the body. There's no choice to leave the body. We have to love it.
>
> That's how it is in the church, too. All of you are the body of Christ, and all of you are necessary for the work of God.*

Don't forget that the real head of the church is Jesus (Ephesians 1:22). Every other part of the body of Christ is equally important— needed as much as anyone else. Some people may think they're the

*Adapted from 1 Corinthians 12:17–27.

brains, but really—how long can they function without what they may see as undercover organs like livers and kidneys that keep the blood supply clean?

God needs leaders. But God's people can only be led in so many directions at one time. And God needs teachers. But we need only spend so much time in the learning mode, and then it's time to act!

Think of the church as a theater. (Not a bad thing to keep in mind because, believe us, people are watching what we do!) In the theater, there's only one director, one conveyer of the vision—that's the gift of *leadership*.

But where would the play be without actors to communicate to the audience? Those are the *teachers, prophets, evangelists*.

And what would happen without technical directors? They're the *administrators* or *shepherds* who carry out the vision.

Can you imagine a theater without set and costume designers? Sound technicians? The hands-on geniuses that create the special effects? In the church, those are the people with the gifts of *helps, mercy, faith, giving, hospitality*. They're not as visible, but they're equally important.

Gifts ≠ Maturity

No parent gives car keys to a newborn. But God dares to give gifts to baby believers. The Holy Spirit gives us power through the spiritual gifts the moment we decide, "Okay, God, I want to be on your team," but we have to grow in smarts and maturity.

Don't assume that just because someone has a flashy up-front gift, he or she has the whole Christian act together. Incredibly gifted Christians do unbelievably stupid and sinful things. People who are really about God's work prove it not just by the *gifts* but by the *fruit* of the Spirit. They are constantly growing in the mature character Paul talks about in Galatians 5:22–23 (esv): "love, joy, peace, patience, kindness, goodness, faithfulness, gentleness, self-control."

Exactly what gifts you discover you have, then, has nothing to do with how mature you are. In fact, it often takes highly mature people to do humble things, which is why Jesus could wash the feet of his disciples. The *gifts* of the Spirit give you the tools to do a job. Growing in the *fruit* of the Spirit allows you to do it in a manner that brings God glory.

Some Assembly Required

Spiritual gifts are like a supercharged gaming computer. The box comes with all the pieces, but you have to put them together. And the more you practice, the better you are at using them. You can pick up tips and new techniques, too, from people who've played the game before. It's the same with spiritual gifts. *Teachers* can always practice their presentation skills and learn more about the Bible. *Encouragers* can grow their listening skills. *Helpers* can hunt down better pancake recipes and practice flipping skills before the next youth breakfast.

As you grow and mature as a person and a Christian, you'll show some ability in most of these gifts. After all, Jesus asks all of us to show *mercy*, to grow in *wisdom* and *knowledge*, to *evangelize*, to *give* of our possessions—so it can sound like we're supposed to have all of the gifts. But some will be more natural for you.

You can see signs of your gifts in things you do easily that are hard or even impossible for your friends.

Maybe you're already teaching your little sibling Bible stories.

Or you're good at spotting right and wrong.

Or you've got the patience to babysit for the overworked parent down the street whose kids *don't* seem to know right from wrong.

Church isn't the only place spiritual gifts show up. You can use your spiritual gifts at home, in school, at a job, with your friends. God can put you to work anytime, anyplace. The key? Knowing which gifts you have so you can put them to use when you see what needs to be done.

Sensational versus Supernatural

Some Christians complain that their gifts seem entirely ordinary. Less than sensational. Maybe even boring. Setting up chairs because you have the gift of helps makes you wonder, *This is so dull—how can it be God using me to do important stuff?* Yet all gifts are supernatural, enabling you to do things above and beyond what you could on your own through your talents. Not all of them are exotic or attention grabbing.

Yes, sometimes God uses eye-popping gifts to get our attention. Especially to make way for evangelism. One youth pastor high-centered a bus—meaning it was hung up with just the chassis, no wheels, touching the ground—with seventy kids on board, two hours from nowhere on a deserted mountain road. (No, it wasn't Kevin.) After the leaders tried everything to get the bus back on the road, the pastor gathered the kids around to pray, "Lord, we're really in a mess, so we could use your help. Amen." BAM! The bus popped free. No one was more surprised than the pastor—but several of the kids accepted Christ on the spot.

You only have to look at the disciples, however, to know that a steady diet of miracles and healings, nice as it sounds, just doesn't get God's true message across. Close followers of Jesus who witnessed all the greatest miracles—like James and John—still didn't get who Jesus was. Peter still temporarily turned his back on God. No, while God has a billion flavors of spiritual gifts, the plain vanilla ones get most of the work done. Vanilla is a great flavor—and versatile. You can add chocolate, strawberries, nuts, bananas, or root beer, using it in dozens of ways. God saves the exotic flavors for special places and occasions.

So Why Unwrap Your Gifts?

Why figure out your gifts? There are two huge reasons. First, there's a lot of work to be done. God doesn't force anyone to use their spiritual gifts. Result? Too many people look around and say, "Hey, not my job!" Whatever your gifts, God set aside tasks within the kingdom that will make a difference and be rewarding for you—tasks that fit your special design.

And that's the second reason to discover your gifts. If you discover the roles God wants you to take on, you can find the spot in God's work where you fit just right. And that's a very cool thing. If service sounds boring, you probably haven't tried the right things yet.

Maybe you've only tried service projects because you had to. Or because you got lured in by your friends. Their idea of fun is refinishing all the chairs in the Sunday school classrooms. You hated it. Give service another chance. You might rather teach the kids who'll sit in those chairs, or take them outside to play Red Rover, or not do anything with kids at all!

So Which Gifts Do You Have?

Remember, if you're a follower of Jesus, the seeds of what you can do for God are already deep inside you. In the years ahead, you'll grow through study and practice in your ability to use those gifts, but you can already begin to discover what they are. Don't worry about which gifts you have. Whatever they are, God chose them just for you. Here's a process for figuring out your gifts:

1. Look through the list of gifts:
   - evangelism
   - helps
   - leadership
   - discernment/prophecy
   - encouragement/mercy
   - faith
   - hospitality/giving
   - teaching/wisdom/knowledge
   - healing/miracles/tongues

Which gifts sound most like you? Start with those "well, maybe . . ." ones as you work through the descriptions of each gift below. Don't miss this: *Then read through the rest of them.* You may be surprised.

2. As you read through a description, think about . . .
   ▸ Does it sound like things you've done?
   ▸ If not, does it sound like things that you might like to do?
   ▸ Is it similar to an interest or ability you already discovered?

3. Decide for yourself whether it might be one of your gifts, scoring as follows:
   1 = Definitely not one of my gifts.
   2 = Not sure. Haven't tried this, but it sounds interesting.
   3 = One of my gifts—I know it.

4. When you're done, transfer your scores here:
   _____ evangelism
   _____ helps
   _____ leadership
   _____ discernment/prophecy
   _____ encouragement/mercy
   _____ faith
   _____ giving
   _____ hospitality
   _____ teaching/wisdom/knowledge
   _____ healing/miracles/tongues

And remember to record your scores on page 236.

The Gift of Evangelism

> The ability to spread the good news of Jesus Christ in a way that appeals to those who don't know him—causing people to accept and follow Jesus.

You may not shout sermons on street corners or carry signs around the school flagpole that say, "Repent!" But you *do* wish that your peers could know your God.

Maybe you wear a necklace or pin with a Christian symbol and can easily tell others about it if you're asked. Or it feels natural for you to invite friends along to events at your church. Or you find yourself thinking about—and then sharing with others—answers to the questions that keep some kids from believing in God—like "Why is there suffering?" or "Is there really only one God?"

Or maybe you're drawn to places where people just don't know Jesus. You can imagine yourself as a missionary—across town or across the world—and hope for chances to share God's good news.

Do you have the spiritual gift of evangelism?

- ☐ I can comfortably talk about my Christian faith with others in a way that makes them comfortable as well.
- ☐ I wish others could understand why my faith is important to me.
- ☐ I enjoy many friendships with people who aren't Christians.
- ☐ I enjoy studying questions that challenge Christianity.
- ☐ I look for ways to help people understand how their needs can be met through Christianity.

Tips on developing your gift of evangelism

1. Study and practice talking about God's grace and forgiveness. It may take some work to figure out your own style and story.

2. Take advantage of short-term mission projects. Talk with people who have done a variety of projects to understand which have the most appeal to you.

1 = Definitely not one of my gifts.

2 = Not sure. Haven't tried this, but it sounds interesting.

3 = One of my gifts—I know it.

Score: _____

The Gift of Helps

> **The ability to work alongside others, seeing spiritual value in the practical tasks that further God's purposes.**

For you, being in the spotlight ranks right up there with a trip to the dentist. And you may not want to attend a bunch of meetings to plan the next homecoming dance.

But—you notice when people need help. You do something about it. And you like it! You don't even have to pause and think about holding a door for someone with too much to carry. You dive in to fold brochures for your mom's business. You put away chairs after youth group. Or find out homework assignments for a sick friend. Or bus tables at a pancake breakfast.

Maybe you've even begun to notice that when you act on these impulses to help others, you give God a chance to act through you. Doing what needs to be done without others knowing it—even before they see the need—lets you be a part of God's work in a meaningful way.

Do you have the spiritual gift of helps?

- ☐ I don't need to be a leader—I'd rather take on practical tasks.
- ☐ I notice little jobs that need to be done and do them.
- ☐ When I help with routine tasks, I feel a spiritual link to the people I serve.
- ☐ Quietly helping others is fulfilling to me.
- ☐ I like working behind the scenes and dislike being praised in public for my efforts.

Tips on developing your gift of helps

1. First, realize that helps is an important gift. In the Bible, the word *helper* is used once to describe Eve, once for King David,

and *sixteen times* to describe God as the source of strong, powerful help. God knows how valuable helping is.

2. Look for people you want to help—leaders, teachers, or others who are active in things that interest you. Speak up about how you might help them. Not everyone sees what needs to be done!

1 = Definitely not one of my gifts.

2 = Not sure. Haven't tried this, but it sounds interesting.

3 = One of my gifts—I know it.

Score: _____

The Gift of Leadership

The ability to motivate, coordinate, and direct others in doing God's work.

Student council, Scout patrol leader, youth convention delegate, team captain—chances are your friends already recognize they can trust you with responsibility. They may even look to you to get things going or to solve a sticky situation, like convincing your confirmation teacher to forget about writing pages of sermon notes each week.

You don't dread being appointed leader of a group. You have enough confidence in your ideas that you can get others to follow your suggestions. Maybe everyone got behind your strategies to tame the neighborhood bully. Or they followed your lead to get ice cream served more often in the cafeteria. Or to get your church to let the teens adopt a nursing home.

For you, it isn't about being a control freak, but knowing that things usually go well when you take the lead.

Note: Two additional gifts are related to leadership: administration and shepherding. Administrators often see the most efficient way to get things done and can organize information, events, or material so things can happen. Shepherds understand how to guide and care for groups of people as they grow spiritually.

People with these gifts may also be leaders. For now, what's most important is recognizing that God might call you to lead in one of these ways.

Do you have the spiritual gift of leadership?

- ☐ Disorganization frustrates me; I want to take over.
- ☐ If I'm in charge, my friends sense we're headed in the right direction.
- ☐ I'm in control of my own time/priorities or my own belongings or finances.

Fitting In with God's Work

☐ I like to organize facts, people, or events.

☐ I can lay out the actions to deal with anticipated problems.

Tips on developing your gift of leadership

1. Work under someone you consider an effective leader—a humble servant of God who motivates others to work together toward a common goal. Find friends who will hold you accountable—those who seem to have faith or discernment—who will help you be a good leader who doesn't abuse power.

2. Study what the Bible has to say about servant leaders. Start with Matthew 20:25–28; Ephesians 2:5–11; John 13:1–15; 1 Peter 5:2–4.

1 = Definitely not one of my gifts.

2 = Not sure. Haven't tried this, but it sounds interesting.

3 = One of my gifts—I know it.

Score:

The Gifts of Discernment and Prophecy

> The ability to recognize what comes from God and what doesn't—or to proclaim God's truths in ways that fit current situations, with insight into how God wants things to change.

You're the one who says, "This isn't right." Maybe you're reading a book, watching a movie, or listening to a speaker and you just know the message isn't what God wants people to hear. Or you're talking with a friend and feel an urge to tell them something about their lives. You see an image of something you didn't dream up on your own—maybe a sunrise or a flower unfolding—and you tell your friend, "God wants to help you make a fresh start!"

Prophets and discerners sense what God wants them to say in a specific situation. Maybe they grasp how an Old Testament Bible story matters for today or what view Jesus might hold on an issue. Usually first, though, they have a strong relationship with God.

Do you have the spiritual gift of discernment or prophecy?

- ☐ I often get a gut feel whether a situation is good or bad.
- ☐ I can judge where people are coming from—whether they're real or fake.
- ☐ I sense whether a book/movie/presentation will bring people closer to God—or push them away.
- ☐ Sometimes I see or think of images that convey God's truth.
- ☐ I listen carefully for what God wants me to say to others.

Tips on developing your gift of discernment or prophecy

1. Study the Bible as much as you can so you understand what God has already told us about a world of issues.
2. Keep a journal where you can record insights, impressions, or images you see and how you are led to apply them. Share

Fitting In with God's Work

103

these with someone who has a mature gift of prophecy or discernment so you can gain their insights.

1 = Definitely not one of my gifts.

2 = Not sure. Haven't tried this, but it sounds interesting.

3 = One of my gifts—I know it.

Score: _____

The Gifts of Encouragement and Mercy

The ability to see the suffering of others and offer comfort by showing empathy, listening effectively, or acting kindly—helping them heal emotionally, relationally, or physically.

You're known as a good listener when friends have problems. Your heart is torn by stories of poverty or illness. And you tend to pick up strays—whether injured animals or kids who have trouble fitting in. They sense they're safe with you.

If you have the gift of encouragement or mercy, you know what to say and do when the chips are down for someone else. Like when a friend's grandma dies—you know whether your friend needs a quiet walk with you or the noisy crowd of a basketball game. You may have felt prompted to sponsor a poor child overseas—and more likely than not, you followed through on that commitment.

Given that one of Satan's nicknames is the *Dis*courager, there's a lot of work to be done by people with this gift.

Do you have the spiritual gift of encouragement or mercy?

- ☐ I get upset when others are hurt or rejected. I want to reach out to them.
- ☐ I like to show others how much God loves them.
- ☐ Others say I'm a good listener.
- ☐ I often see the best in others—things they're slow to recognize in themselves.
- ☐ I see how I can help others and can gain their confidence easily.

Tips on developing your gift of encouragement or mercy

1. Take a class in peer counseling or peer mediation.
2. Find a mentor with these gifts. Go with them to pray and minister to those in need of help.

3. Get active in or financially support "mercy ministries" to help those less fortunate than you—feeding the hungry, building homes for the poor, helping in development work.

1 = Definitely not one of my gifts.

2 = Not sure. Haven't tried this, but it sounds interesting.

3 = One of my gifts—I know it.

Score: _____

The Gift of Faith

The ability to recognize what God wants accomplished—a strong belief that God will see it done no matter how big the barriers.

You "know" when God wants something done—healing a relationship, empowering people to start a new program, or providing funds for you to join on a mission trip. Even when the odds are stacked against it and people say, "It can't be done," sometimes you can see that God is going to pull it off anyway. Long ago your friends stopped trying to talk you out of things you're confident about. Now they just call you a hopeless optimist.

Maybe it was your conviction that your church would let you paint murals all over the old sanctuary walls. Or that your youth group could raise enough money to purchase a van to haul senior citizens to Sunday services. Or your vision of how a service project might get pulled off, right down to your knowing the kind of sandwiches the church would provide for the trip.

Prayer for you is acknowledging that God is active in our lives.

Do you have the spiritual gift of faith?

- ☐ I know God is faithful, even when life seems impossible.
- ☐ I firmly believe God is active in our lives.
- ☐ My friends tell me I'm an "incurable optimist."
- ☐ If I sense that God is behind a project or idea, I can support it even when others are doubtful.
- ☐ My personal experiences help me believe in the power of faith.

Tips on developing your gift of faith

1. Pray with other people who have the gift of faith.

2. Record instances of when you are sure God is at work. Reread them later to see what actually happened. How often were you right?

1 = Definitely not one of my gifts.

2 = Not sure. Haven't tried this, but it sounds interesting.

3 = One of my gifts—I know it.

Score: _____

The Gift of Giving

The ability to give of material possessions freely and happily to assist people and further God's causes.

Instead of having a long wish list of things you want to buy, you're aware of how much you already have. Maybe you even feel a bit guilty when you ask your parents for better shoes or new clothes. But that guilt pushes you to think of ways to do what you can for those who have less.

Perhaps you agreed to give up fast food for a year to help sponsor a child overseas. Walked or ran for breast cancer. Willingly gave of your clothes and shoes when another family lost everything in a fire. Packed baskets for a Thanksgiving food drive. Or you seemed to know which adults might provide financial support for a mission trip. You had no trouble approaching them successfully.

Or it's important to you to set aside some of your allowance or what you earn for a cause you believe in. Maybe it already isn't enough to rest on what your parents give—you want to help, too. And you feel connected to the person or organization you support. It's one way you really feel a part of what God is doing.

Do you have the spiritual gift of giving?

- ☐ I handle money well.
- ☐ No one has to push me to give to others.
- ☐ It's easy for me to ask others to give to causes I believe in.
- ☐ I've had ideas that helped my family give more money to others.
- ☐ Giving to a cause or ministry helps me feel a part of it.

Tips on developing your gift of giving

1. Study what the Bible has to say on money and possessions. Start with Luke 21:1–4; Luke 12:16–34; Matthew 6:19–21, 24; 1 Timothy 6:6–11; 1 Peter 5:2–4.

2. Research the causes that interest you. How might you free up money to give to them? Remember, it isn't *money*, but the *love* of money that is the root of all evil. Some very wealthy people have this gift—they look at each dollar they earn as a dollar available to fund others to carry out God's purposes.

1 = Definitely not one of my gifts.

2 = Not sure. Haven't tried this, but it sounds interesting.

3 = One of my gifts—I know it.

Score: _____

The Gift of Hospitality

> **The ability to demonstrate God's love by providing others with a warm welcome, food, shelter, or fellowship.**

You know how to make other people feel welcome. Everyone wants to sit at your lunch table because you steer the conversation so everyone's at ease. You adjust the chairs so there's room for late arrivals. You share your dessert.

If there's a new student around, you're the first to invite him or her to join your crowd for a movie or to sit together at the next basketball game. You don't want anyone to stay a stranger for long.

And your friends like to gather at your house—not necessarily because you have a pool or the best video games, but because you know how to make them feel comfortable.

You know that it's pointless to tell someone about God's love if you don't take time to know them, if they don't trust you, or if they feel unwelcome. You work hard to create a safe space that makes others feel important.

Do you have the spiritual gift of hospitality?

- ☐ I can make all kinds of people feel welcome.
- ☐ I make an effort to connect with new people at church or school.
- ☐ I seem to know what activities or food will appeal to others.
- ☐ If I help with arrangements for a party or event, I think less about what I want than what will make others feel welcome.
- ☐ I see relationships as opportunities to pass on God's love.

Tips on developing your gift of hospitality

1. Don't worry if you don't have a huge space for entertaining or you can't afford to order pizza from the best delivery place

in town. Some people offer hospitality to huge crowds, others to just a few people at a time. The important thing is whether you and your guests feel comfortable.

2. Create ways to work with your group at church or clubs at school so that more people feel welcome.

1 = Definitely not one of my gifts.

2 = Not sure. Haven't tried this, but it sounds interesting.

3 = One of my gifts—I know it.

Score: _____

The Gift of Teaching

The ability to understand and communicate God's truths to others effectively—so that truth changes lives.

You're interested in learning about God, the Bible, and how your faith can help you day to day. Maybe you've memorized key Bible verses that explain your values and morals to others. Or you read books by Christian authors in your spare time—with no one making you.

If you're listening to a teacher, you might automatically think of other examples or ideas that would help make the point clearer. Sometimes when you're reading a Bible story, you start imagining what you'd like to tell others about it and even how you'd present the lessons you learned.

You may already be teaching younger children. Maybe you help your little sister work the puzzles in her Sunday school paper. Or you tell stories while babysitting or help with a class at a local preschool or vacation Bible school. You want children to understand how important God is to you so they can develop their own faith.

Note: The gifts of wisdom and knowledge have many of the characteristics of teaching. *Wisdom* is the ability to apply God's truths to difficult problems. *Knowledge* is the ability to understand and use information that might come from natural sources or straight from the Holy Spirit.

Teens often have trouble recognizing these gifts in themselves, sometimes because they don't want to be proud and sometimes because they feel like no one will listen anyway. If you feel like you have a gift of teaching, wisdom, or knowledge, continue to cultivate the wisdom that you'll gain in the school of life's hard knocks. And pay attention to what James says: "Who is wise and understanding among you? Show by your good life that your works are done with gentleness born of wisdom" (James 3:13 NRSV).

Do you have the spiritual gift of teaching?

- ☐ I enjoy studying the Bible and other resources that help me learn about God.
- ☐ I like to learn about new ideas, gathering information so I can pass it on to others.
- ☐ I want to relate God's truth to life in a way that helps people grow and develop—not to skewer them with truth but to help them.
- ☐ When I study or hear other teachers, I automatically think about how I might teach the information to others.
- ☐ When I talk about what I've learned, others often want to learn more about God.

Tips on developing your gift of teaching

1. Take advantage of opportunities to study and share the Bible with others. Volunteer as a camp counselor or church school or preschool aide, or simply work with others you know well—your siblings or friends. How exciting can you make the materials?

2. Even if you have the gift of teaching, study teaching methods either through classes or by observing your favorite teachers, noting why they are so effective.

1 = Definitely not one of my gifts.

2 = Not sure. Haven't tried this, but it sounds interesting.

3 = One of my gifts—I know it.

Score: _____

— The Gifts of Tongues, Healing, and Miracles —

> The ability to function in ways that are unexpected and even miraculous—not for the sake of bringing attention to yourself but in order to demonstrate God's power.

Chances are you haven't walked on water lately. Or brought anyone back from the dead—and no, waking up friends during an incredibly boring chemistry lecture doesn't count. But obviously supernatural gifts still operate today. We don't always listen well to what God has to say, so God still occasionally pulls out all the stops to get our attention. These gifts are like a wake-up call, holy alarm clocks so we don't miss the real message.

Tongues: In the second chapter of the book of Acts, the apostles—after being filled with the Holy Spirit—spoke to the crowds so that everyone heard the speeches in their own languages. Elsewhere, the Bible tells us that if someone speaks in the "tongues of angels" someone else needs to interpret what they are saying. Some studies show that when modern-day people speak in tongues, they aren't just making up nonsense but are using words that fit language patterns—but words that aren't from any earthly language.

If you never speak in tongues, don't worry. God doesn't command us to. Paul said he'd rather speak five words of good teaching than ten thousand words in tongues (1 Corinthians 14:18–19).

What's most important is letting God influence your life through the Holy Spirit however *God* wants.

Healing: It would be easy if we had a God who *always* heals or *never* heals, but we have a God who *sometimes* heals. Why some people are healed is a mystery, but healing is best understood as yet another way God shows love to us. When healing is made more important than other spiritual gifts, God's love gets lost. Those that aren't healed may feel God somehow loves them less. True healers focus attention on God, not themselves. They listen to the sick to hear their needs and often want to pray for them. They celebrate the healing of relationships, of spirit, and of the mind as well as physical healings. Most of all, they try to listen to God in each situation, seeing their prayers as acts of obedience to God.

Miracles: Miracles are happenings that don't happen in the normal course of life. They bust natural laws, demonstrating God's power over nature, matter, disease, or life itself. Do miracles still happen? Some people spend their lives looking for natural explanations or coincidences to discount all miracles. Yet if you talk to enough people, particularly ones involved in helping people find God—and especially as missionaries or others on the front edge of the expansion of God's kingdom—you'll probably hear too many stories of miracles to dismiss them all as coincidences. If you have faith that miracles happen even today, who knows what you might see. . . .

1 = Definitely not one of my gifts.

2 = Not sure. Haven't tried this, but it sounds interesting.

3 = One of my gifts—I know it.

Score: _____

Where Do You Go from Here?

1. *Test your spiritual gifts.* While reading about spiritual gifts may give a clue as to how God wants to use you, in the spiritual realm there's no room for armchair theoreticians. Acting on your gifts will let you assess whether you've correctly identified them. If you want God to help you spot your gifts, get out and do *something*. After all, you can't steer a parked car, and you can't know where God wants you to go without giving your life some gas.

2. *Practice, practice, practice.* Just like life gifts, spiritual gifts take practice—ask anyone who's tried to talk about her or his faith. While in one sense spiritual gifts are dropped on us by God, experience often makes the difference between bungling and breaking through with God's love. Experience makes your gifts work in the real world.

3. *Look for formal and informal opportunities to serve.* People with the same gifts may find wildly different arenas to apply their skills. Formal ministries—through your church or other organizations—can offer you training and access to people with well-developed skills. Informal ministries—reaching out on your own or with a friend or two—let you apply your gifts all day long. One size doesn't fit all.

4. *Look for things to do inside and outside of the church.* If you're a follower of Jesus, you know that your faith applies to more than churchy things on Sunday mornings or Wednesday nights. The only way to extend God's kingdom and demonstrate God's love to the world is to exit the warm confines of the church and enter the world of everyday life. School, work, socializing, and family relationships are all places to give with the gifts God gave you.

5. *Don't exercise your gifts alone.* You wouldn't want to take on the eleven members of an enemy football squad all by your lonesome. You can't take on the world's problems all on your own. Get connected to a church—both peers and adult Christians—who can work with you to spot and sport your gifts.

5

Choosing Your Path

Values

Assume for a moment that you just took a job at a pet store. And pretend it wasn't because your parents barked, "You can pay for your own gas or you can't drive the car." Working was *your* choice. So why work? And why this job?

Maybe you took the pet shop job because you value *friendship*—and you'll be working with your best friend.

Or because you value *leisure*—and this place shuts up by 7:00 p.m. weeknights and never opens on Sunday.

Or you value *learning*—you're mulling a career in veterinary medicine and you want the animal expertise. Especially the part where you clean up after the puppies.

Then again, maybe *adventure* and *independence* were key issues for you—you've heard that the owner hires just a few people she can trust and then lets them run the show, paying well for high responsibility and performance.

Add *flexibility*, *balance*, *stability*, and more to your possible reasons.

Sometimes you're cornered into taking a job because it's the only thing you can find. Often, though, you have the chance to choose, to make a decision based on more than dimes and dollars. In some circumstances it feels like you're adrift on a wide-open ocean. So which way do you sail?

Valuing Your Values

Finding your fit depends on spotting what we've already looked at—interests, abilities, spiritual gifts—plus one more topic we'll get to in the next chapter, personality. But there's another part of finding your fit that helps not just in picking jobs but in navigating all of life: values. Values are your ideals. Your principles. Your inner model of what a sails-hoisted-high, both-oars-in-the-water, steering-by-God's-stars kind of person looks like.

And that's the biggest value of values: If you understand your values, you're on the fast track to making smart life decisions. Whenever you have a decision to make, it challenges you to either stick to your values or veer away. If you choose in ways that keep you on course, you'll feel confident about some of the biggest issues in your life.

Values aren't the *things* on your wish list like a Maserati, a personal jet, or a horse ranch. They're the *ideals* that determine who you are and shape your life.

- ▸ Values reveal what matters to you. Would you rather take a class that's *challenging*—and where you know you'll probably mess up—or stick to subjects where you know you'll be *competent*?
- ▸ Values define your bottom-line character. What can other people count on you for? You can offer them *integrity, perseverance, stability*.
- ▸ Values make work and life meaningful. Would your life be dull or even hopeless without *friendship* or *creativity* or *achievement*?

- Values guide your decisions. Choosing a college is easier if you know that you value *prestige* over *location*—or vice versa!

- Values compel you to take a stand. Values define lines you won't cross. You push back if you discern a lack of *fairness* or *generosity* or disregard for *tradition*.

- Values help you determine where and how you can live, work, and serve. They tell whether in the scheme of things you need *adventure, personal development, variety, influence.*

You might not be able to consciously identify your values until you pause, sit down, and purposely figure them out. And your values may not always stay the same! Down the road, things that happen in your life might lead you to value something more or less than you used to. But your goal is to discern what you value right now—and in a moment you're going to tear some cards out of the back of this book and figure out for yourself what you value most.

Sometimes you don't realize how much you value something until it gets called into question. The biggest test of values comes when you run headfirst into a values conflict—when an event, person, or situation upsets you enough to realize your values are telling you to act differently than others do.

Value Clash Ahead

You might think of a conflict of values as a clash of morals—like being asked as a Christian high schooler to sing a choir piece that seems to mock your faith (happened to Kevin) or being assigned books to read that grossly offend your moral standards (happened to Karen). For sure, values are about these deep *good-and-evil* dilemmas—deciding what media you'll consume, how far you'll go on a date, or whether to help people by donating some of those pet shop earnings.

Those clashes involve values and choices, but those are actually the easy ones. Like we said earlier in the book: Scripture clearly marks off many boundaries between good and bad. No need to wrangle over what's in bounds and what's out.

Making up your mind to obey those unchanging commandments of God will get you through half of the values decisions you face. But there's another half. Sometimes, you'll need an ability to pick between two *good* things. Both halves are important to pleasing God. Both halves are important to living life well and making smart decisions.

Let's just say you're soaring through life like a massive jet. Without both wings, you'll fall from the sky. Wing one: the skill to choose between right and wrong. Wing two: the ability to pick between good, better, and best:

- ▸ Your schedule won't let you go out for both the cross-country ski team and dance in the school musical. Do you ski—or shuffle?

- ▸ A friend wants you to share an apartment after you graduate. You'd planned on staying at home for a few more years. The plot thickens when you get only a few hours to sign on the dotted line of a rental agreement—or not. What then?

- ▸ You want to spend your summer as a camp counselor—outside, having fun, not making a whole lot of money—and your parents think you should be a security guard for much bigger bucks an hour in some stale warehouse. What to do?

The more you know about your values before these conflicts happen, the easier it is to make the right choice. And the true worth of knowing your values comes as you face even huger decisions of life:

- ▸ Maybe you're in the middle of the great education dilemma. "You don't know how lucky you are to have the chance to go to college," says your aunt. But your neighbor claims that college degrees are pointless: "They'll make you pay to take art history.

What good is art history going to do you? Now, plumbers or computer technicians—they'll never be out of work."

▶ And once you decide between college and trade school, you have to pick a major or specialty. So where you gonna work? Live? What will you do with the money you earn? Your spare time?

Before you lapse into unconsciousness worrying about the future, check out the power of knowing your values.

Choose or Lose

Alec had two claims to fame in high school: (1) sculpting, and (2) being able to fix anything with a crank, gear, or ball bearing. He barely survived chemistry and trigonometry, so he had no intention of taking premed classes. But ever since his cousin lost a leg in a ski accident, Alec dreamed of somehow *serving* others, not as a doctor but by gaining *competency* somehow in the area of physical therapy or coaching special needs kids in sports. When his advisor suggested a trade school that ranked first in the field of designing and fitting artificial limbs, Alec jumped for it. It blended his artistic gifts with his desire to put them to practical use. Because Alec knew what he valued, he was ready to act when he saw an opportunity.

Or take Kim's struggling to choose between two short-term service opportunities. One involved outdoor construction work, which matched her values for *physical fitness* and *nature*. The other meant working on a musical production, which matched her values for *artistic expression* and *creativity*. Both were good choices, but Kim analyzed how her top values would be affected in each situation. Kim sensed that the first one might allow her to develop deeper *friendships*. That swayed her decision.

In a nutshell, values help you answer the big questions: What's a meaningful life?

What will I do with my time?

My money?

The gifts and talents God gave me?

And where do I take a stand?

Choose What You Value?!?

Wait a second. At this point you might be saying, "Don't I have to value things like *relationship with God, family*, and *service*? Isn't that Christian? What do you mean, 'Choose your values'?"

Look at the different values cards in the back of this book. You'll see that we aren't looking at bad values—tormenting small animals or tossing people off the corporate ladder as you scratch your way to the top. This isn't even like academic ethical discussions where you decide who in the lifeboat should live or die. This is about understanding the core of what makes you tick—the things you value most highly, the things you can contribute to others. You're about to consider what you want other people to say about you. For example:

- ► People counted on George Washington's *integrity*.
- ► Everyone knows Gandhi stood for *peace*.
- ► Michael Kors lives for *aesthetics*.
- ► Tarzan couldn't swing through the jungle without *nature*.

Get it? Values are the compass you use to steer through life.

Checked and Double-Checked Choices

If you don't know where to start, look at what drives people you know.

There's nothing wrong with *achievement*, for example, if you understand what God wants you to do with success. And you don't end up worshiping yourself or money instead of God.

Some of your friends thrive on *competition*—it spurs them to their best efforts. That's fine with God, too, so long as you're still a good loser. And you don't sabotage your competitors.

Others have to be *challenged*—they seek out problems or interests that no one's tackled before. That's great as long as you can still be responsible. And you don't neglect the mundane areas of life.

Plenty of people dream of how they can somehow make a *contribution*—an idea or a book or a cure for some disease that has an impact on others. If the end result doesn't honor God, though, it's the wrong value. (Just think about the books that God no doubt wishes had never been written.)

Indispensable Values

Unlike your interests, abilities, spiritual gifts, and personality, God doesn't just hand you your values. You do get some choice. God influences those choices, but other than some foundational precepts, the choice is up to you. It's part of the flexibility God built into the planet.

Yes, we're all to put God first in our lives. Sometimes looking at values helps you see if you're really doing that. Where does your *relationship with God* fall on your list of top values? Be honest.

Yes, we're all to love our neighbors as ourselves. But we can do that in different ways. Who do you know that shows love through *fairness? Generosity? Service? Loyalty? Peace? Responsibility? Artistic expression?* Love comes in a variety of shapes and forms—and we have the freedom to choose how we love our neighbors.

If your values allow you to honor those don't-mess-them-up commandments, the next step is determining what other ideals you need to lead the life God designed for you. There's one important question: Do the values you've picked help you fulfill God's purposes for you? *That's* the kind of guidance you want from values. If you're steering with the right values for the right reasons, you've got a plane with both wings. You'll end up at your destination: a life pleasing to God.

Ready for Solitaire?

Time to do a fun values sort using the cards in the back of *Find Your Fit*. Go ahead and tear out the values cards now. Each lists a separate value. Note that there are also blank cards if you think of a value we didn't include.

The exercise is easier done than said:

1. Find a place where you can lay out all of the cards.
2. Place the big prompt card ("If I had complete freedom and responsibility to make my own decisions, this is how I would value _____.") at the very top of your work space.
3. Place the medium-size heading cards ("These are very valuable to me," "These are valuable to me," "These are not very valuable to me") in a row underneath the prompt card.
4. Filling in the blank on the prompt card with each value, quickly sort the values cards into the appropriate columns, laying them out so that you will be able to view all of the cards in one glance. Do this *rapidly*, following your feelings or instinct rather than trying to analyze each one thoroughly.
5. Place no more than eight cards in the "These are very valuable to me" column. This could be a difficult task!
6. Next, rank the cards within the "These are very valuable to me" column, placing the value that is of most importance to you at the top of that column.
7. Copy the values in the way you have sorted them onto the Values Summary Page (127). You will now have a record from which to complete the exercises.
8. Record your top eight values on page 236, "All about Me."

Values Summary Page

Copy the values from your sorted cards onto this page in the order you gave to them. This will give you a working record to use for the exercises. (You don't have to order the second or third columns, but it can be helpful to record which values you put in each column.)

These are very valuable to me	These are valuable to me	These are not very valuable to me

Acting out Your Choices

Of course, living by your values isn't quite as simple as just sorting cards. Once you choose them, you have to *own* them, *breathe* them, *act* them out. Not just react once a situation passes and you realize you blew it.

King David had all of his values down pat—and wrote them out for all of us to see:

- ▶ *Relationship with God:* "I have set the Lord always before me" (Psalm 16:8 ESV).
- ▶ *Loyalty:* "Who may dwell on your holy hill? Those who . . . stand by their oath even to their hurt" (Psalm 15:1, 4 NRSV).
- ▶ *Generosity:* "Happy are those who consider the poor" (Psalm 41:1 NRSV).
- ▶ *Integrity, responsibility:* "For I have kept the ways of the Lord, and have not wickedly departed from my God" (Psalm 18:21 NRSV).

So where were all of David's ideals when he saw Bathsheba the bathing beauty up on the rooftop—and had her husband killed so he could take her as his wife? He tossed them over the parapet and lived for the moment—a moment he paid for the rest of his life. And while any of us is just as capable of making mistakes, the more time you spend owning your values, the more likely they are to jump in front of your brain and yell, "STOP!" if you're about to make an unwise choice.

So you need to figure out your values before you back yourself into a corner or decisions surprise you. But—if you don't choose the right values, you won't make the right decisions. Your values need to line up with who God meant you to be, because they influence every area of your life.

Peeking around the Corner of Life

While your interests, abilities, spiritual gifts, and personality are more constant, your values need constant scrutiny. Life changes.

Your priorities shift. Your responsibilities don't stay the same. We'll assume that right now you place a fairly high value on *learning*, but once you finish school you may not. Some people find that their zest for *adventure* lessens once they're married with two kids and a mortgage. Pity the family where parents don't learn to put a high value on *responsibility*. And in forty years you could be the cranky oldster who values *nature* to the point that you yell at neighbor kids to get off your lawn.

What's the next season of your life? Define it below for yourself—new school, different location, summer job, college or technical school, major, job applications. What new values might you hold and why? Which do you need to downplay or ditch—like the desire to play away four years at college? Re-sort the cards to see if there are any differences.

The next chunk of my life will be _____.

My current values	My top eight values for the next season of my life—and jot a note why
1. _____	1. _____
	_____
	_____
2. _____	2. _____
	_____
	_____
3. _____	3. _____
	_____
	_____

My current values	My top eight values for the next season of my life—and jot a note why
4.	4.
5.	5.
6.	6.
7.	7.
8.	8.

The shifting values in the varying seasons of your life often boil down to timing. You might choose to demote a value in favor of one that you need to promote for that chunk of time. Go back to the pet shop job. Maybe you've worked at the Adorable Puppies Pet Shop for three years and you're trying to convince Mom and Dad that a summer mission trip or college semester abroad is the growth experience you need. They think you need the income. Can you use your values to talk with them about long-term goals? Is there a big future payoff—maybe not financial gain but for personal development or experience—that would sway their decision? How can you meet the needs of their values *and* yours?

Jane did it by giving up being on the swim team—not a huge loss to the world of sports but a compromise to her value of physical fitness—so she could waitress her tail off during the school year. Her earnings funded her summer studying in Malta. During high school, Kevin—by agreeing to stay home and work his next summer vacation—bargained with his parents to let him go on a summer mission trip to Canada. Karen spent an entire summer squinting at boring spreadsheets in order to earn money to buy her first car and drive it to college.

One final question: What steps might you take now to be sure you can live by the values you'll need in this next season?

Owning Up to Your Values

You're in a time of life when you need to own your values more than ever. Getting clear on what you value can prepare you for that next chunk of life—like Cassie and her mother found out:

> "You're not going out with a twenty-two-year-old, and that's final. He's a man, you're a teenager, and I'd be failing you as a mother if I said yes," Cassie's mother said.
>
> "But, Mom, you know Christopher is trustworthy. You had friends on the committee that chose him to work at church," Cassie argued. "Besides, he's only three years older than me, just like you and Dad."
>
> "I didn't date your father when I was nineteen. And that's the end of this discussion."
>
> Just then Cassie's older brother, Tyler, walked in. "Mom, you probably won't like what I'm going to say, but think about it. Cassie leaves for college in two weeks. The campus is filled with twenty-two-year-olds for Cassie to date, and your rules won't apply. You have to start trusting her judgment, because in two weeks' time you won't have any choice."

Cassie thought she was old enough to choose whom she wanted to date—and given her changing circumstances, she'd better be. She needed room to make her own choices, yet she'd be stupid to chuck her mom's values unthinkingly.

So what's the problem? Neither she nor her mother had thought through the responsibilities Cassie would face in college. Cassie still relied on her mother's rules and values. She hadn't been in many situations where she had to grapple with her own decisions. As she and her mom went back and forth, she realized she valued her *family* and her *purity* just as her mother did, and she also wanted to keep her *self-respect*. She needed to figure out how she and her mom would meet her need for *independence* and *flexibility*.

You may be looking forward to making all your own decisions. Problem is, it's easy to get so caught up in dreaming about what you'll do "when I make my own rules" that you end up short on time to make those choices well.

Fortunately, no one—least of all God—expects you to arrive at adulthood with the wisdom of the ages. You're going to learn from mistakes, messed-up priorities, and harmful relationships. And when you do, try using your values as a tool to figure out what went wrong. What values did your decision or the situation reflect? Did it cause you to rethink what you value? Have your priorities changed, or did the mistake show you that something else has a much higher value?

And if you've practiced . . . practiced . . . and practiced some more making decisions with your values in mind—you'll be ready.

Putting Your Values to Work

As you step into the next stage of your life, your values will steer you in all kinds of decisions—the big and small, from major ethical dilemmas all the way down to deciding which class to take next term. When Karen sits down with students planning for college, she hears a lot about the values they have (whether they know it or not!). If you watch for it, you'll see how your big-picture values play out in very practical ways.

- ▸ One person says she wants "a college where no one else from my high school goes." She craves some *adventure*.
- ▸ Another says he wants to find "a school that won't bury me in debt." He's thinking about *financial security*.
- ▸ Some students want to get into "a college that everyone knows is great." They want to go somewhere with some *prestige*.

Values show up all the time in career choices, too! When you're investigating all the things you could do "for the rest of your life" (that's a myth, by the way), you'll find that your values sit up and start talking. Most teens don't have concrete ideas about what they want their work to be like until they start comparing their options head-to-head, so do your research about the careers you're considering, and you might find that your values make the decision easy!

- ▸ How would you feel about a job that keeps you on your feet all day? It might work for those who value *physical fitness*, while others would want a job that lets them sit and focus on what they're doing because they value *accuracy*.
- ▸ How about work that has you talking with different people all day? That sounds like heaven for some people who value *cooperation*, but for people who want some *independence*, it would be way too much.
- ▸ Or what would you think about a job that puts you in charge of a whole group of people? For some, that kind of *advancement* is exactly what they've always wanted. But for others, moving up into that position would be way too big of a change. They want *stability* in their work.

When you start looking, you'll find there's a lot of career options out there, and they are wildly different from each other. Just think about how different a day in the life of a bank manager is from the day of a forest ranger! You might be faced with choices between jobs in completely different parts of our economy—or maybe a choice between two in the same career field. The difference between a bank manager's and a loan officer's day is much smaller, but still significant. All these decisions get easier when you start noticing what your values and preferences are about the way you want your work to be.

Job Giveaway

Look over the two jobs below. Don't play "guess this job"—just pay attention to what the jobs are like. If someone was giving these two jobs away, which one would you want?

Job #1	Job #2
► You will make $60,000 per year. ► You must spend at least two to five years in higher education to qualify for this position. ► You spend the majority of your time in a clinic or hospital. ► You will wear a uniform most of the time. ► You often provide advice and emotional support to people you don't know well. ► You will analyze medical tests and results. ► You will administer treatments and medications. ► You will spend considerable time walking, bending, lifting, and standing. ► You will work closely with others on a team. ► You will deal with blood and needles, and you will have close contact with strangers' bodies.	► You will make $125,000 per year. ► You must spend seven or more years in higher education to qualify for this position. ► You spend the majority of your time in an office. ► You must dress nicely for your job at all times. ► You have to remember and keep track of a lot of important information. ► You read many long documents that you must analyze carefully. ► You must make very important decisions that affect others' lives. ► You spend a lot of your time listening and writing, sometimes talking or giving speeches. ► You will often need to work and think independently. ► You will need to continue taking courses to further your education.

1. What appeals to you about the jobs above? Go back and circle anything from either job description that you like.

2. What don't you like about the jobs above? Go back and cross out anything that makes you hesitate (or makes you want to puke!).

3. Would you take either of these jobs if they were offered to you? Why or why not?

We could play this game all day, because the world is full of interesting occupations. (Dying to know what those jobs are? A nurse and a judge!) The job you'd rather take is a better reflection of your values—can you see why? And if you want neither, then you'd better keep looking!

One of the biggest challenges that people your age deal with is an overwhelming number of career options to decide between. It's a good problem to have and a *privilege* that most people in the world don't have. But it's still a problem, and it can stress you out. In order to keep your head from spinning, you've got to get some real-world information stuffed in your brain so you know what you're deciding between! Then you can sort out which options to follow up on and which ones to forget about. It's called e-*valu*-ation, deciding between things based on your values.

If you come into college or into the workforce with a pretty clear understanding of what you want and WHY, you will be so far ahead of other people your age. The WHY is the part that helps you sleep at night—you're able to settle into your decision because you know why you made it and why it makes sense. That adds up to something invaluable—peace of mind.

Where Do You Go from Here?

1. *Check out which values you sorely lack.* Think of some tough situations you've faced. Could you avoid a repeat by paying more attention to a value that isn't in your top eight? Some

people lose friends through a lack of loyalty. Some can't get a deserved break from a teacher because they showed a lack of responsibility in the past. Maybe God wants you to pull a different value to the top.

2. *Compare your values with those of your peers.* Conflicts over values aren't just about sex standards. What roles do values like *competition, adventure, physical fitness, conformity*, and *control* play in your relationships—look through all the values to see which others bring up issues where you haven't gotten along with friends. How could you resolve conflicts based on your values?

3. *Consider the values your parents hold.* If you can, let your parents sort the values cards themselves. See how many of your top sixteen you have in common—after all, you are in different stages of life. Where you differ, take time to think about whether you've chosen your values wisely. To get the conversation off to a positive start, you might want to first show them your value list and how they guide your decisions. Don't make this an opportunity to push your agenda, but do some heartfelt learning about your parents.

4. *Compare your values with those of someone you admire.* What values do you think they hold? How do they differ from yours? Any changes you want to make?

5. *Look at your values through the eyes of others.* Would they say that your actions reflect your values? If they sorted the cards for you, how would they rank your values?

6. *Look at your values in terms of work settings.* Where could you work that would click with your values? What characteristics would your job need to have? Creativity, for example, is honored in advertising—not in accounting. If you like nature, concentrate on jobs that don't require living in Manhattan. Brainstorm with your friends on what your values mean for both volunteering and work.

7. By the way—in case you lose all those nifty tear-out cards—the list of values to sort is on page 237!

6

Finding the Places You Fit

Personality Type

You can't read minds. And maybe that leaves you wondering what some of your friends really think. For example: Some tell you all about their problems. Others could be dying inside and never say a word.

Or you're amazed to see how people treat other people. Like how they handle getting asked out. Some can't stand to say no because they don't want to hurt anyone's feelings. Others don't even pretend to make up an excuse—they just say no.

And it's bewildering to watch friends do life so differently. When you plan a party, for instance, Ashley wants to invite half the school, while Jen thinks a group of three or four sounds great. Friends tease Josh for planning who brings what in advance, but Nick just tells everyone to bring whatever they want, taking the chance there won't be enough to go around. Emma tells you a party sounds great, but later you find out she wanted to do something else—but didn't want to raise a fuss. Tyrone, just the opposite, tells you up front what he wants to do—a group hike gets a yes, bowling a no.

What Does It Matter to You?

Even when you and your friends gather around a shared interest like sports, music, church, or afterschool stuff, you aren't clones of each other. Even if you have a huge assortment of *many* commonalities, look closer. You aren't as much the same as you seem. You have distinct likes and dislikes in how you live. In how you relate to your friends. In how you make decisions.

Those kinds of preferences are what your *personality type* is all about.

Imagine you're about to punt a football. Do you have to ponder which foot to use? No. You naturally prefer one or the other. Or do this scribble test: Sign your name below with your preferred hand, the one you always write with:

_____

That was easy. Normal. You don't have to stop and consciously engage your brain to form the letters. But try it with your other hand:

_____

Not quite the same! Clumsy. Hard. Like picking up Jell-O with chopsticks. Of course, if you've ever broken your preferred hand, you know it's possible to improve clumsy wrong-handed writing. But it takes effort.

It's the same with personality. People have different preferences that go way beyond being a lefty or righty. Look at your friends. Who tells the whole lunchroom they found a dollar on the bus—and who wouldn't let on even if they'd won the lottery? Who can you count on to plan a great ski trip—and who just lets things happen?

You can easily tell who's left- or right-handed. Or who uses their left or right eye to look through a microscope. Those physical differences are easy. With practice, though, you can start recognizing your inner or psychological preferences, too. You're born with preferences for

- getting energized by the outside world or by what's inside your head (Extraversion versus Introversion)
- paying more attention to details or to the big picture (Sensing versus Intuition)
- making decisions with your head or with your heart (Thinking versus Feeling)
- planning your life or going with the flow (Judging versus Perceiving)

Understanding your preferences helps you understand why some situations feel natural for you and others make you squirm. Or why you can have such major misunderstandings with some people. Or why you can or can't be set in stone about some issues—and much more.

Square Pegs for Square Holes

Personality type describes major, *naturally observable differences* in normal people. Nearly a hundred years ago, Swiss psychologist Carl Jung and, independently, Americans Katharine Briggs and Isabel Myers came up with similar frameworks for how people act and interact. Their efforts were popularized through the Myers-Briggs Type Indicator® (MBTI), the most widely used personality test in the world today. Chances are that your parents, teachers, or youth leaders have taken it.

Businesses use the MBTI to help create better teams.

Schools use it to understand how students learn best.

Marriage counselors use it to cut through couples' communication problems.

Individuals use it for self-awareness, acceptance, and direction.

Here we're focusing on giving you clues to recognize places you'll fit in—where you'd enjoy volunteering, learning, working, or even playing.

Warning: As you start this section, think about only yourself and what you truly prefer. Not what you think would help you make friends. Not what your parents or teachers think you *should* do.

Not what people tell you it takes to get ahead in the world.

No type is better than any other—just different. So concentrate on what fits you best. After all, God certainly didn't give human beings just one personality model. You can prove that to yourself by thinking about Martin Luther, Mother Teresa, and C. S. Lewis for a moment. Pretty different people, yet each has been used by God.

With that said, let's find your preferences. We'll look at each of the four areas mentioned above to get a better picture of you.

Energy—from Others or from Inside Your Head?

Think about the places you went yesterday.

Extraverts get charged up by being with others. They're drawn to people, events, and activities—the outside world. If they try to do something alone, they may feel lonely and brain dead. *Anywhere* there's action or other people is better than sunning on the beach alone. One Extravert said, "I'd rather talk to the chair than just sit by myself." You don't have to be a party animal to be an Extravert, but if you get your energy from

- being with others *or*
- pursuing a variety of activities

chances are Extraversion describes you.

Introverts get recharged by connecting with their own thoughts, feelings, ideas, and awareness—their inner world. They're more

Finding the Places You Fit

comfortable doing things by themselves. And after high-intensity time with others—like a day at school—they like nothing better than to crawl to their rooms, put on their headphones, and settle in with screen time, books, or a hobby. Introverts aren't hermits, but think about this: Is it as easy for you to run alone as with a friend—or would you just as soon play with the cat or read a book as call up a friend? If you get your energy through

- time you enjoy away from others *or*
- a few in-depth activities

you may be an Introvert.

Extraversion or Introversion isn't about shyness. Shy people can still be Extraverts who like the outer world of people and action. They just may want more of the same people and familiar faces. (The spelling difference—it's "extr*a*vert," not "extr*o*vert," the word we use in everyday conversation for a loud, outgoing person—is meant to point this out.) Introverts can still be the life of the party—they just need more space, more time on their own.

As you go through the following either/or scenarios, you might see yourself on both sides of the fence. But try to get a handle on which way you'd choose most often if you were just being yourself. (Remember, it's easier to operate outside of your preferences if you *know* you're out of your element.)

1. You find out a group is going to the beach. Which sounds more like you?

Extraverts might . . .	Introverts might . . .
☐ call up lots of friends to make sure they're going	☐ agree to go if you know one other friend is going
☐ sit with different people throughout the day, enjoying being part of a big group	☐ stick with one or two close friends for most of the day

Extraverts might . . .	Introverts might . . .
☐ eat and visit with a big group as you roast hot dogs and marshmallows	☐ roast your hot dog, then pull away from the big group to chat with just a couple people
☐ jump in with a joke or new idea if there's a lull in conversation	☐ get lost in thought when there's a lull in conversation
☐ join the group for volleyball, water polo, the limbo, water-skiing, or whatever else you can	☐ join the group only if you've tried the activity before or if one or two of your close friends join you

2. You're supposed to work with a group on a school project. Which describes your approach to the assignment?

Extraverts might . . .	Introverts might . . .
☐ have fun working as a group, scheduling joint trips to the library, etc.	☐ divide up the assignment so you can do your part alone
☐ call a friend to talk through ideas	☐ think through ideas alone
☐ turn the group sessions into a chance to socialize	☐ keep the group sessions shorter unless working with a close friend
☐ share ideas readily	☐ share ideas when asked
☐ leave the group sessions full of energy, ready to go out for burgers	☐ be ready for solo time after longer meetings

Summing Up

Extraversion	Introversion
☐ doing; lots going on	☐ reflecting; one thing going on
☐ find interruptions refreshing	☐ find interruptions distracting
☐ outgoing	☐ protective
☐ invite others in	☐ wait to be invited
☐ say what you're thinking	☐ keep thoughts to yourself
☐ outer energy	☐ inner energy
☐ act	☐ reflect
☐ live it first	☐ understand it first
☐ focus outside	☐ focus inside
☐ take over	☐ step aside

If you still aren't sure which preference best describes you, think about how you like to do your homework. Would you rather sit at the kitchen table where there are lots of interruptions? Work with study partners? Find yourself wanting to be with friends even though you've been together all day long? If so, you may be an Extravert.

Or do you want to retreat to your room for a while after school, maybe turning on music as background to keep out other distractions? Would you rather work through your homework on your own? If so, you may be an Introvert.

If you still can't decide, that's okay—it takes time to work out all four of your preferences.

Circle which describes you best:

E (Extraversion)   **I** (Introversion)   **X** (Not sure yet)

Taking in Information—What Do You See?

People with a preference for *Sensing* pay attention to the information gathered through their five senses. They process facts, sounds, sights, textures, and details. They know *what is*. At school, they like subjects where you know whether you're right or wrong. Math— where two plus two always equals four. Spelling—where you either memorized how to spell s-e-p-*a*-r-a-t-e or you didn't. Fill-in-the-blank reading assessments—where you either know the information or you don't.

People with a preference for *Intuition* pay attention to their hunches, connections they make, or analogies they can draw. They know *what could be*. Intuitives rely on their sixth sense more than the other five. At school, they'd rather use their imaginations than stick to the facts—and may be accused of daydreaming or wandering away from the subject at hand. They might want to write their own ending to a story, and enjoy tests that require analogies ("Shakespeare is to John Green as Einstein is to _____"). They may even get annoyed if a teacher makes assignments too specific.

Put yourself into the following scenarios to see whether Sensing or Intuition is your preference.

1. Your teacher assigns a report on Greek mythology. How would you tackle it?

Sensors might . . .	Intuitives might . . .
☐ want to know the rules—how many pages, which references to use, printed or in Google Docs, etc.	☐ want to know the possibilities—can you write a story, design a game so others can learn the names of the gods, put on a play?
☐ ask for a list of suggested topics	☐ brainstorm your own topic, then ask for approval
☐ want to know the requirements for an A, B, or C grade—and do what you have to for the grade you want	☐ write what you want, not worrying about the requirements if you find the topic interesting
☐ regurgitate the facts you know the teacher wants	☐ find new information on related topics you discover
☐ choose a topic where you know you can give the "right" answers, the facts ("Food Mentioned in Greek Mythology")	☐ choose a topic where you can write on themes, analogies, or general concepts ("Echoes of Greek Mythology in Modern Soap Operas")

2. You're with a group of friends at lunch, discussing what you did over the weekend. How would you describe your days?

Sensors might . . .	Intuitives might . . .
☐ start by telling what you did Friday night, then continue, in order, to Saturday morning, afternoon, evening, etc.	☐ start with whatever comes to mind first, then jump around from day to day
☐ relate facts about where you went and what you did	☐ jump from the facts to ideas you had or what you might like to do next
☐ stick to what happened ("I had pepperoni pizza—next time I might try it with mushrooms")	☐ use what happened to bridge to far-out topics or fantasies ("We ate pizza out under the stars and I thought, *What a great scene for ending a movie.*")
☐ describe an event in detail— directions for how you got there, what you ate, who you met	☐ describe an event by comparing it to other events, stating generalizations or conclusions about what you saw
☐ fill your weekends with tried-and-true activities you enjoy	☐ try to find new things to do or experience

Summing Up

Sensing	Intuition
☐ practical, common sense	☐ innovative, insightful
☐ accuracy	☐ creativity
☐ use past experience for current work	☐ use inspiration for current work
☐ methodical approach	☐ new, innovative approach
☐ by (or buy!) the book	☐ create the book

Sensing	Intuition
☐ current reality	☐ future possibilities
☐ stick with it until you're done	☐ stick with it until you find a better way
☐ real world	☐ ideal world
☐ applied	☐ theoretical
☐ identify pieces	☐ identify connections

If you still aren't sure whether Sensing or Intuition best describes you, think about how you handle details.

Sensors can often put things back exactly where they found them (the cookies were on the second shelf, right-hand side of the cupboard), while Intuitives may have only a vague notion of where they got it (the cookies were in the cupboard). Sensors may remember exactly what their date wore Saturday night; Intuitives may have trouble remembering whether they wore shorts or a suit. Sensors can give detailed directions on how to get to their house or school; Intuitives may refer to landmarks or use phrases like, "Drive for five minutes or so until you see a stop sign."

Circle which describes you best:

S (Sensing)   **N** (Intuition)   **X** (Not sure yet)

Decisions—How Do You Make up Your Mind?

Everyone makes decisions, but we use different criteria. *Thinkers* use their heads—they rely on logic and impartial standards—and are quick to poke holes in each alternative. Thinkers live to argue—they can take either side of an issue just to test their logic. They want fairness and may choose to be truthful rather than tactful. You might hear them talk about pros and cons, goals and objectives.

Feelers use their hearts—they rely on their values and the needs of others, putting themselves into the shoes of each person involved. They may find it easy to talk about the good side of each alternative and agree with what others want. Feelers often make exceptions to rules if they see a need for compassion. You might hear them talk about values and personal meaning.

Both Thinkers and Feelers use *rational* processes to make their decisions, but school teaches us to focus on logic and standards. To

Finding the Places You Fit

better understand Feeling, consider times when you thought rules should be bent—like when you broke curfew because your friend forgot to put gas in his car. Or when rules should be firm—like when half the class stayed home all weekend to finish an assignment and the other half starts whining for an extension because they went to the beach. Getting inside people's heads to understand their reactions makes sense.

How might you react in the following situations?

1. Summer is coming, and Mom or Dad says you have to find something to do—either a part-time job or a volunteer position to keep you busy.

Thinkers might . . .	Feelers might . . .
☐ set goals or objectives for your summer activities	☐ decide what might be meaningful to you for the summer
☐ decide on objective criteria—hours, pay, store discounts	☐ check out what your friends are doing and see if you can join them
☐ choose something that will add to your résumé	☐ choose something that allows you to help people
☐ use logic to analyze your choices	☐ ask for opinions from others about the choices
☐ concentrate on the flaws in each choice	☐ concentrate on the positive points in each choice

2. It's the start of a new school year and time to meet all the new teachers. How do you separate the good teachers from the bad?

Thinkers might . . .	Feelers might . . .
☐ look first for what's *wrong* with the teacher (dress, organization, quality of assignments)	☐ look first for what's *right* with the teacher

Thinkers might . . .	Feelers might . . .
☐ judge a teacher as smart or stupid based on minimal input ("If that's all she knows about Lincoln's second inaugural address, she doesn't know history")	☐ develop alternative explanations for why a teacher may be struggling ("She must not have been feeling good")
☐ be concerned with how competent the teacher is	☐ be concerned with whether the teacher likes you
☐ want information presented in a logical, concise manner	☐ want information presented in a personal way
☐ prefer clear standards and goals for a class	☐ prefer that the teacher treats students as individuals

Summing Up

Thinking	Feeling
☐ logical, analytical	☐ harmonious, personal
☐ ideas for data and things	☐ ideas for people
☐ fair but firm—few exceptions	☐ empathetic—making exceptions
☐ business first	☐ friendship first
☐ recognition for exceeding requirements	☐ praise for personal effort
☐ analyze	☐ sympathize
☐ impartial	☐ subjective
☐ decide with the head	☐ decide with the heart
☐ find the flaw	☐ find the positive
☐ reasons	☐ values

If you are still undecided, consider what you do when friends tell you about problems they're having. Thinkers often analyze the situation and offer advice, even giving opinions on what their friends did wrong so they'll avoid making the same mistakes. Feelers may offer sympathy and even focus on what their friends did right.

Sometimes Thinkers and Feelers don't even speak the same language—("I don't *think* you should have done that"; "Well, I don't *feel* that way at all").

Circle which describes you best:

T (Thinking) **F** (Feeling) **X** (Not sure yet)

Planning—Work before Play or Go with the Flow?

Somewhere in middle school or thereabouts, you were given more responsibility for completing your homework and chores. As you grew up into that newfound freedom, you probably noticed your friends approached life in one of two ways. *Judgers* (who are *not* judgmental—we've got a different meaning here) plan their work and work their plan. They dig in on assignments so they can hang out with friends knowing it's all done. They don't pull all-nighters, and they just seem to know how much time a task will take—"How can you sleep if all that work's still hanging over your head?" Judgers hate wasting time or being late. They make decisions quickly and stick to them—trying on sweaters, for example, only until they find one they like enough to buy.

Perceivers (who are *not* more perceptive) take advantage of the moment. If it's a nice day, why would you do homework before shooting hoops? After all, the weather could get worse—"How can you concentrate when the sun is shining?" They may not work on an assignment until they feel inspired. Perceivers may arrive "just in time" more often or change plans more easily. They may postpone decisions until they gather more information—trying on sweaters in lots of stores before buying one.

How might you act in these situations?

1. It's Friday, the weekend's coming, and everyone is grabbing stuff from their lockers and heading out the door. How do you approach the two days ahead?

Judgers might . . .	Perceivers might . . .
☐ consider the time available and schedule exactly when you'll do your homework	☐ do your homework when you feel like it—or last thing Sunday night because you didn't get around to it earlier
☐ feel guilty "playing" before your work is done—maybe even checking off your list of things to do	☐ forget about your work or find ways to work and play at the same time, ignoring your list of things to do—if you even bothered making one
☐ study the TV or movie schedule and plan your day so you can watch a certain show	☐ turn on the TV and flip channels when you feel like it
☐ make set plans for Saturday with a friend before leaving school on Friday—plans guarantee a good time	☐ start calling friends sometime Saturday and go wherever with whoever's available—plans might keep you from a better option
☐ complete your homework from start to finish	☐ skip the hard parts in homework so you keep going, maybe even leaving the toughies until Monday's free period

2. You're about to buy a new "toy"—fresh tech, a guitar, or a new video game. How do you go about making a decision?

Judgers might . . .	Perceivers might . . .
☐ limit how long you'll spend shopping	☐ shop as long as needed to check out all the options
☐ decide in advance which models or games you'll try based on price, features, or other set criteria	☐ try as many models or games as you can, not wanting to tie yourself to criteria in advance
☐ quickly narrow down the selection from many choices	☐ be overwhelmed by too many choices, find it hard to limit your options
☐ reach your decision quickly—even before you have all the facts	☐ get as much input from friends and experts as possible—even postpone your decision
☐ not second-guess your choice once you've bought it	☐ revisit your decision if you find out new information

Summing Up

Judging	Perceiving
☐ organized, efficient	☐ flexible, multiple tasks
☐ planned events	☐ serendipitous events
☐ reduce stress by planning ahead	☐ reduce stress by having options
☐ settled and decided	☐ open to late-breaking information
☐ work before play	☐ work and play coexist
☐ regular, steady effort leads to accomplishment	☐ much is accomplished at the last minute
☐ systematic	☐ spontaneous

Judging	Perceiving
☐ scheduled	☐ spur of the moment
☐ definite selection	☐ several possible choices
☐ enjoy finishing	☐ enjoy starting

If you still aren't sure whether Judging or Perceiving describes you, think about ordering at a restaurant. Judging types tend to decide quickly among burgers, pizza, or salads and then make a fast decision. Perceivers look over the whole menu, check out what people ordered at the table behind them, ask the waiter what everyone's raving about, and may not decide until it's their turn to order.

Circle which describes you best:

J (Judging)   **P** (Perceiving)   **X** (Not sure yet)

Your Personality Type

Congratulations! You've made it through all of the preferences. Now put the letters you chose to describe you in the blanks below to record your four-letter personality type. Don't worry about placing an x in one of the blanks if you're still not sure.

$$\text{E}_{\text{or}}\,\text{I} \qquad \text{S}_{\text{or}}\,\text{N} \qquad \text{T}_{\text{or}}\,\text{F} \qquad \text{J}_{\text{or}}\,\text{P}$$

Type Frequently Asked Questions

Figuring out your personality type is often a brain-busting experience. The type description pages coming up may peg you so well that you wonder if the researchers bribed your mother to tell them what you're really like. Or you may feel annoyed that you're not what you'd like to be. Things to think about:

Is everyone born a certain type?

Your type was most likely part of how you were hardwired at the baby factory, but type can be influenced. If most of a family is Introverted, the lone Extravert may learn to be quiet. If your parents are Thinkers, you may get a lot of practice in logical debate even if you're a Feeler. If that's the case, it may take a while to figure out what God meant you to be.

Are all people in one type alike?

No. They have more things in common than with people of other types, but type doesn't explain everything. Kevin, Karen, and Jane are all INFJs. We're all writers, we play the guitar, love to read, work best on our own, and make most deadlines. But Kevin bikes, Karen walks, and Jane runs. Kevin did his master's degree in theology, Karen in counseling, and Jane in business. Kevin hates board games, Jane willingly plays everything from Candy Land to

Pandemic, and Karen can't stand cards but beats everyone in Trivial Pursuit. Balance all that with our shared faith in Christ, and we have worldviews similar enough to easily set common goals for writing and working together.

Can I change my preferences?

You can work on sharing your thoughts. Or being organized. Or walking in the other person's shoes. But first, celebrate who you are. No type or preference is better or best, just different. Focus on your strengths, not your weaknesses. If we're all gifted—but in different ways—then the best type to be is your own. When you work on your weaknesses, don't be discouraged by the fact that it's a battle to change. Everyone struggles. We just each struggle in different areas.

My type description says I have trouble being on time—or being accurate, tactful, etc. Can I use my type as an excuse?

Absolutely not! You can't use your personality type to excuse inexcusable behavior. Instead, use type to figure out what coping skills might help you in life. Perceivers might try setting deadlines for each step of a report instead of focusing on the final deadline. Introverts might work harder to share their ideas. Look ahead to the pages for your type; we included those "Hints for Getting Along in Life" ideas because type helps people see rough spots to smooth out in how they get along at work, at home, at school, with friends, etc.

Should I base my career on type?

No. Don't use type as the only factor. Even if you research a career and find out most people in that profession have a different type, pay more attention to the tasks you'd do, the people you'd work with, and the work setting. If the career still appeals to you, go ahead. Sometimes being an oddball gives you a different perspective that is priceless to your co-workers. And knowing in advance that you're different is way better than wondering why you don't fit in.

What does the Bible say about personality type?

Lots. Well, sort of. Carl Jung, not Moses, was the first person to write about psychological type. You might wonder whether people change personalities once they become Christians and are therefore "new creations in Christ Jesus."

While no specific biblical reference can be used to prove or disprove type, we can easily point to evidence in the personalities of major Bible heroes. For example, remember the apostle Paul—first introduced in the Bible as Saul.

Saul, action-oriented and outspoken, probably had preferences for Extraversion. He led crusades against Christians, with letters from the high priest in hand granting him license to kill.

With his big-picture approach to destroying the church, we'd guess he had a preference for Intuition. His training in law and deep scholarship as well as credibility with the authorities point to a preference for Thinking. And his decisive manner suggests a Judging lifestyle.

After conversion? Paul tranformed from the biggest persecutor of Christianity to its biggest promoter. But notice how much he was just like the old Saul: He employed flawless logic in writing letters to churches (Thinking). He was driven to travel and preach (Extraversion). He had a global approach to issues the young church faced (Intuition). And he showed whopper decisiveness in debate (Judging). You can argue—and some people do—that Paul was an ENTJ or ENTP, depending on how you read the clues. But one thing is certain. While Paul's *values* and *beliefs* changed, he kept his ENT personality that made it natural for him to lead and persuade others.

So Where Do You Go from Here?

1. *The rest of this chapter contains descriptions of each personality type*—ways people of each type prefer to learn, how they communicate, surroundings they prefer. If you're undecided about your type, look at the pages for possibilities to see what

describes you best. If you wrote ESxP above, for example, read the pages for ESTP and ESFP. Highlight the parts you can relate to. See if you can find yourself.

2. *Think about your life.* Type is all about figuring out what comes naturally to you. It's your chance to understand why some things come easily and why others are frustrating. What situations are comfortable? Distressing? Any clues why? One teen finally learned why group projects bothered him so. As an Introvert and a Thinker, his best thoughts came when he was alone. Still another learned why taking over the family store sounded so ghastly. Her dad was a Sensor who enjoyed the routine of his days. She was an Intuitive who craved new experiences.

3. *Think through your relationships.* Review what you checked off as you learned about preferences and look at the page for your individual type. As you learned about Extraversion and Introversion, Sensing and Intuition, Thinking and Feeling, or Judging and Perceiving, did you have any *aha!* moments about how you fit—or don't—with your friends, your parents, or your school? Do you see any places where you obviously clash? One girl discovered she was a Thinker and confirmed that her mom was a Feeler. They put an end to many disagreements when they balanced their needs for fairness and kindness.

4. *Read more about type.* Especially if you aren't yet sure of your type, here are two great resources:

   ▸ *LifeTypes* by Sandra Krebs Hirsh and Jean Kummerow (Warner Books, 2009).
   ▸ *Creative You: Using Your Personality Type to Thrive* by David B. Goldstein and Otto Kroeger (Atria Books, 2013).

   Your local library may have them. Both contain true-life stories.

5. *Learn from your opposite.* Look at the type page for the type most different from you. For example, we INFJs would look at the ESTP page. Sometimes seeing this very different picture can clue you in to what you need out of work and service.

6. *Highlight the "Hint for Getting Along in Life" that strikes home most.* These tips all came from adults who learned the hard way about their fatal flaws. Think of the last time things didn't work out the way you wanted or you messed up a relationship or fell short of expectations. Be honest. Would following any of these hints have eased the problem?

7. *Enrich other areas of your life with type.* If type opens your eyes to who you really are, the following resources can help you learn more:

   ▸ *Do What You Are* by Paul D. Tieger, Barbara Barron, and Kelly Tieger (Little, Brown, 2014). A great book about type and careers.

   ▸ *SoulTypes: Matching Your Personality and Spiritual Path* by Sandra Krebs Hirsh and Jane A. G. Kise (Augsburg Books, 2006). Describes the soulwork that fits each type as well as factors that can hinder spirituality.

   And dozens more. That's why we're introducing you to type. Check out the topic at your local library and you're bound to find more on type in the world of business, on teams, in school, in relationships . . . more stuff than you can read in a lifetime.

8. *Remember to record your personality type* on page 236, "All about Me."

ISTJ

A thunderous round of applause for ISTJs—
they keep the rest of us organized!

What you're known for

▸ being practical and sensible—doing what's expected and what's worked before

▸ doing what you said you'd do—you mean it when you make a commitment

▸ working steadily—setting and sticking to schedules and goals

▸ liking order and structure—wanting to know the rules, and at ease when people follow them

Top career choices

▸ accountant

▸ computer professional

▸ dentist

▸ electrician

▸ math teacher

▸ manager/administrator: government, corporate, small business

▸ mechanical engineer

▸ police supervisor

▸ school principal

College and career tips

▸ It's normal for your type to approach the college search practically—checking out two-year colleges to save on tuition, staying closer to home, etc.

▸ You'll probably be most comfortable choosing majors or trades that lead to solid job markets and career stability.

▸ Know that the study habits that worked in high school may not work in college; make use of writing centers, study sessions for freshmen, etc.

▸ Remember to plan time to relax and have fun—and date. That's all part of the college experience!

Where you learn best

▸ when you can apply the information—it's practical and relevant

▸ when the materials are precise and accurate—you might get skeptical if they're too fluffy or play fast and loose with facts

▸ when objectives and standards are spelled out so you can judge for yourself when you've mastered the material

▸ when materials are presented systematically and logically

Where you'd prefer to work or serve

▸ working on your own, uninterrupted

▸ doing hands-on projects where you can see results and know when you're done

▸ with people who pull their own weight—or else you do it all out of a sense of duty

▸ on organizing, financial, or record-keeping tasks that are structured and orderly

How you lead people

- by setting an example of hard work and follow-through
- expecting rules to be followed—traditionally, top-down style
- focusing daily on immediate, practical needs
- taking a no-nonsense approach, often picked to lead because of reliability
- using past experience and the facts of a situation to make decisions

Hints for getting along in life

- Make exceptions—understand when and why rules might be bent.
- Notice the forest—step back from the details of a decision or situation, look for the big picture or long-range results.
- Open up to others—share your special sense of humor and express your appreciation.
- Be flexible—try new methods or experiences, try to understand other points of view.

ISTPs . . .
get energized by the inside world
look for the facts
decide with the head
go with the flow

A thunderous round of applause for
ISTPs—they get rid of red tape!

What you're known for

▸ being an in-depth expert—pursuing as much skill and information as you can in the things you love

▸ working efficiently—getting around the "rules and the fools," assessing which shortcuts will be tolerated

▸ having a few close friends—avoiding the "social butterfly" scene

▸ enjoying independence—setting your own goals, disliking routine

Top career choices

▸ information technology specialist

▸ construction worker

▸ dental hygienist

▸ electrical engineer

▸ farmer

▸ mechanic

▸ military personnel

▸ pilot

▸ probation officer

Finding the Places You Fit

College and career tips

- ▶ You love to keep options open, including career choice. Focus on general required courses your freshman year and investigate majors that offer stable, hands-on careers.
- ▶ Know that few professors think and learn like you do. They may not present materials as clearly and logically as you'd like.
- ▶ Use study resources on campus to help you move from facts to the bigger picture.
- ▶ If you tend to underestimate how long things will take, start planning backward from the due date so you start soon enough.

Where you learn best

- ▶ at your own rate through hands-on experiments and experiences
- ▶ in subjects that focus on facts, logical rules, and systematic problem-solving techniques—wrapped together with a practical application
- ▶ when you don't have to rely heavily on imagination or dwell too much on theories
- ▶ with teachers who help you find shortcuts—or know enough to get out of your way

Where you'd prefer to work or serve

- ▶ helping out in different crises—flood and other kinds of disaster relief
- ▶ using your practical life gifts—building, repairing, organizing things, etc.
- ▶ through athletic or outdoor-oriented ministries or organizations
- ▶ through set tasks that don't require a lot of planning or meetings—lawn or building maintenance, cooking, driving, etc.

How you lead people

- providing your own expertise and hardworking example
- supervising only when others don't follow through, treating everyone as equals
- basing decisions on logic and your own set of guiding principles
- focusing on efficiency, practicality, perseverance, and flexibility
- leading if you can't accomplish a task alone or are convinced your knowledge is essential

Hints for getting along in life

- Listen to your feelings and the feelings of others—you might tend to ignore them in favor of principles and logic.
- Aim for effectiveness, not just efficiency—in rushing to find shortcuts or do away with red tape, you may undervalue a process or look lazy.
- Follow through—analyze tasks you have a hard time completing and learn to finish the important ones.
- Plan ahead—in your focus on the practical, you may ignore what will help you long-term.

ESTP

ESTPs . . .
get energized by the outside world
look for the facts
decide with the head
go with the flow

A thunderous round of applause for ESTPs—
they help the rest of us enjoy life!

What you're known for

- adding fun and excitement to life—inviting others to go where the action is
- being energetic—preferring any activity or adventure to abstract learning or sitting still
- staying calm in a crisis—easily spotting the practical tasks that can be accomplished
- telling it like it is—seeing the facts, pointing out the truth, catching the joy of the moment

Top career choices

- auditor
- business manager, small business owner
- carpenter or construction worker
- community health worker
- craft worker
- farmer or landscape architect
- law enforcement
- marketing or sales professional
- pilot

College and career tips

► Seek an environment that includes experiential learning if possible—you're at your best doing, not taking a test.

► Seek "real world" majors that require action and flexibility, not tons of theory.

► Study groups may make hitting the books more attractive, but monitor whether you're turning sessions into playtime.

► Learn to focus in on key information and ideas for studying and before you begin writing; you may need to study with a buddy to do this.

Where you learn best

► when you see the direct payoff for learning about something

► in situations where expectations are clear and realistic

► in subjects that apply to one of your interests, stick to the facts, and have consistent rules

► from teachers who are engaging and can fend off boredom—plenty of variety, hands-on activities, and practical applications

Where you'd prefer to work or serve

► working with people of any age in activity- or adventure-oriented ministries or organizations

► where you can make a contribution and have fun at the same time

► in the moment—when you can show up, finish an assignment, and be done

► hands-on tasks, disaster relief, one-time efforts where you can see tangible results

How you lead people

► by finding the quickest and most direct way to move a task along

- getting others to buy into your point of view by negotiating and persuading
- bringing order out of chaos, handling distractions well
- focusing on immediate results, on action instead of discussion
- taking charge in a crisis, doing what needs to be done with superb timing

Hints for getting along in life

- Think before you speak—you can see flaws so clearly, but others may not be ready to hear them.
- Look at your own role in a problem—you may blame others before considering your part.
- Plan before acting—especially for big decisions, put a lid on your tendency to plunge ahead.
- Balance work and play—you may talk about your hobbies so much that people think you don't have job skills.

ESTJ

ESTJs . . .
get energized by the outside world
look for the facts
decide with the head
live by a plan

A thunderous round of applause for ESTJs—
they take charge and get things done!

What you're known for

► leading—you can tell others how to accomplish something, know step by step what to do, and dig in yourself to help

► being decisive—using logic and past experience to critique choices, then making up your mind quickly

► following through—you stick to your commitments and principles

► having your act together—you set goals and plan to meet them

Top career choices

► government worker, administrator
► insurance agent or underwriter
► small business owner
► manager or school principal
► military personnel
► nursing administrator
► police officer
► sales representative
► teacher: trade or technical

College and career tips

- If you're a quick decision maker, slow down and rethink your choice of schools and careers. Don't lock in too soon!
- Careers that let you be in charge and lead to tangible results may be most attractive to you.
- Know that the path to success in many college courses isn't as clear as you may like.
- Learn to trust your hunches on abstract test questions—your type usually scores lower if you revisit questions.

Where you learn best

- by the book, in line with a schedule so you can plan ahead
- when expectations, objectives, and constraints are clear—you know *exactly* what you have to learn and why it's important
- through experience—experiments, field trips, group activities
- from teachers who are fair, give clear assignments, and maintain discipline

Where you'd prefer to work or serve

- as a leader or administrator
- direct, tangible projects where you can clearly see the need you're meeting
- with hardworking, goal-oriented people who are efficient and stick to schedules
- where you can lend your experience and organizational skills to problem areas

How you lead people

- automatically—you take charge quickly and provide structure, direction, and focus
- using your principles, logic, and past experience to make decisions quickly

- setting goals, modeling efficiency and responsibility
- assigning tasks and giving advice—top-down, traditional style
- seeking measurable results, focusing efforts to make progress

Hints for getting along in life

- Listen to others—you're great at convincing people that your way is right, but you need their perspective more than you may think.
- Stop and smell the roses—remind yourself of this: When I'm sixty-four, what will I have missed by being too goal-oriented?
- Don't just think about the task at hand but concentrate on people—they may work even harder if you consider their needs and reward their efforts.
- Examine your life—are you succeeding not just at school and work, but in family and personal relationships, your spiritual walk?

> **ISFJs . . .**
> **get energized by the inside world**
> **look for the facts**
> **decide with the heart**
> **live by a plan**

A thunderous round of applause for
ISFJs—they're as good as gold!

What you're known for

- being dependable and responsible—keeping things in order and honoring commitments
- helping others—with sensible, daily, behind-the-scenes tasks
- avoiding the spotlight—joining traditional activities or clubs instead, making a few close friends for life
- studying and working—putting work before play, showing self-discipline

Top career choices

- family practice physician
- accountant
- clerical supervisor
- curator
- librarian
- medical technologist
- nurse
- preschool and elementary teacher or aid
- religious professional

College and career tips

- It may be natural for you to wish to stick closer to home than your friends and to value job stability as you make your school and career choices.
- Studying alone is great, but get help or find a study partner rather than trying so hard on your own that you stress out.
- Schedule time to play—join some activities, make regular time for friends, and relax once in a while.
- Seek opportunities to trust your hunches and imagination— you have a wonderful creative side.

Where you learn best

- when subjects have clear, right answers that allow you to demonstrate how hard you've worked
- from teachers who appreciate your efforts and with whom you feel a personal connection
- through organized lectures about concrete subjects, with explicit outlines and set learning objectives
- in situations where following the rules allows you to achieve results you can be proud of

Where you'd prefer to work or serve

- out of the limelight, calmly and efficiently
- with conscientious people who are as responsible and caring as you are
- through practical, defined roles—hospital volunteer, club treasurer, etc.
- in ways that you can use your life gifts to help people directly (listening, attending to detail, writing, organizing, teaching, etc.)

How you lead people

- ▸ taking charge reluctantly, usually only if someone asks you to
- ▸ encouraging others to do their best, promoting cooperation and kindness
- ▸ organizing others conscientiously and quietly to complete tasks efficiently and by the book
- ▸ concentrating your detail orientation to accomplish practical results
- ▸ picking up the slack if others don't, out of a sense of duty

Hints for getting along in life

- ▸ Stop doing other people's work—*tell* them to follow through on what they promised.
- ▸ Pay attention to your own needs—you'll have more to give to others if you do.
- ▸ Take the credit you deserve—tell others what you've accomplished, especially if they thought they did it without you!
- ▸ Set priorities—instead of working through things in the order they came your way, decide what is most important to you and others.

ISFP

ISFPs . . .
**get energized by the inside world
look for the facts
decide with the heart
go with the flow**

A thunderous round of applause for ISFPs—
they teach us to be compassionate!

What you're known for

- helping quietly—directly meeting the needs of others
- being kind—knowing just what to say and do at just the right moment
- appreciating this life—seeing the hand of God in the beauty of nature or the little things around you
- creating harmony—helping others cooperate by the way you model compassion and gentleness

Top career choices

- veterinarian
- carpenter
- elementary teacher
- nurse
- office manager
- physical therapist
- police detective
- surveyor
- X-ray technician

College and career tips

▸ Keep your options open for college choices as long as you can, as well as your choice of career, but make sure you're actively evaluating which might be best and why.

▸ Know that few professors are your type. Don't let that stop you from feeling that you can be successful.

▸ Take advantage of opportunities to learn time management and study skills. This can be a great way to boost your confidence.

▸ Join up with the service organizations on campus that connect with causes you value.

Where you learn best

▸ when subjects are relevant—not abstract, not even traditionally academic

▸ in situations where the structure allows for your spontaneity

▸ through hands-on activities such as building models, experiments

▸ when learning about people and how to help them

Where you'd prefer to work or serve

▸ meeting the needs of individuals directly—nursery, preschool, those with special needs, elder care, etc.

▸ practical tasks that clearly help others

▸ behind the scenes, with others who cooperate and seek harmony

▸ on artistic efforts that will appeal to the five senses—what people will see, hear, smell, etc.

How you lead people

▸ taking charge reluctantly, only when no one else will or your knowledge is crucial to an effort's success

▸ being considerate, compassionate, tolerant, and forgiving

- praising others, not criticizing
- taking responsibility by following through and keeping track of details
- remaining flexible, open to the needs of the moment and the people around you

Hints for getting along in life

- Deal with conflict—instead of sweeping it under the rug, use it to clarify your needs and those of others.
- Recognize your own value—turn down your self-criticism and see the gifts God gave you.
- Establish boundaries—give others opportunities to help themselves. You can't do it all!
- Be assertive—your needs and desires are important, too.

> **ESFPs . . .**
> get energized by the outside world
> look for the facts
> decide with the heart
> go with the flow

A thunderous round of applause for ESFPs—
they're fun and friendly!

What you're known for

- being friendly—everyone enjoys your company
- adding enthusiasm—your fun-loving nature adds zest anytime, anywhere
- giving—you willingly share your time and talents with others
- providing energy and optimism—you look for the positive in life, look past people's flaws

Top career choices

- athletic coach
- child care worker or preschool teacher
- graphic, interior, or landscape designer
- factory or site supervisor
- office manager or receptionist
- public health nurse
- religious educator
- respiratory therapist
- marketing professional

College and career tips

- You're the type most likely to hope to attend a college that a friend has also chosen. This is fine, but make sure it fits your goals.
- Seek opportunities for experiential learning; your brilliance often shines in the lab or in practical problem-solving rather than on tests.
- Watch your socializing:studying ratio.
- Studying with others may help you stay focused, engaged, and more flexible in reading between the lines for test taking.

Where you learn best

- through group projects where you can build relationships while learning
- when the atmosphere is harmonious and inclusive
- if you know your teachers well and they take a personal interest in you
- with minimal independent reading or quiet study of theoretical matters

Where you'd prefer to work or serve

- doing tangible acts for others—decorating, driving, caring for children
- planning and helping with celebrations, gatherings, and parties
- youth, young adult, sports, and action-oriented ministries
- visiting with the elderly or the sick

How you lead people

- using your enthusiasm to get others excited about a task
- gaining consensus, seeking input from everyone before making a decision

- emphasizing teamwork, helping people work together harmoniously
- being warm and relationship-oriented, winning the cooperation of others
- adapting to changing circumstances, reacting effectively in a crisis

Hints for getting along in life

- Determine your own needs and values—you may hide your preferences to keep harmony.
- Balance the roles you play—do people only see you as "everyone's friend" or do you show your gifts and talents?
- Pinpoint your priorities—in your efforts to help everyone and bring enjoyment to all, you might not take time to plan for the future.
- Nurture your spiritual side—your wonderful spontaneity may cause you to neglect God.

ESFJ

> **ESFJs . . .**
> **get energized by the outside world**
> **look for the facts**
> **decide with the heart**
> **live by a plan**

A thunderous round of applause for ESFJs—
they make the rest of us feel welcome!

What you're known for

- working for harmony—wanting everyone to get along and fit in
- following through—staying organized and keeping your promises
- helping out—seeing what friends need and doing the right thing
- accepting structure—unless traditions or rules are heartless

Top career choices

- family physician
- child care worker
- dental assistant
- elementary or secondary schoolteacher
- home economist
- nurse/nurse administrator
- office manager or receptionist
- religious educator
- speech pathologist

College and career tips

- Visit campuses and classes—you'll do best where group work, class discussions, and students helping other students are the norms.
- Use your natural organizing abilities to set your study schedules, but investigate study-skills help if classes seem too "intellectual" for your taste.
- While you naturally reach out to help friends, make sure you're also meeting your own needs.
- Enjoy participating in campus groups. Consider which ones might give you some hands-on experience before you lock in on a career.

Where you learn best

- in structured situations where you can schedule and complete your work
- when you like your teachers and understand their expectations
- from teachers who offer praise, not criticism
- through group experiences (unless distracted by friendships)

Where you'd prefer to work or serve

- organizing others to get something done, from social events to food shelf drives
- hospitality responsibilities (welcoming, decorating, social activities, etc.)
- visiting with senior citizens, shut-ins, the sick, etc.
- with people who are conscientious, sensitive, and appreciative

How you lead people

- taking charge yet taking care of others
- building relationships before tackling tasks

- including everyone in each decision, inviting others to help out
- setting an example of hard work and follow-through
- keeping things organized, on schedule, and by the rules

Hints for getting along in life

- Listen to others—you may be better at *telling* them what they need than *hearing* their needs.
- Recognize your needs—you may be so willing to help others that you wear yourself out.
- Keep some things private—occasionally say less than you know.
- Balance tasks and people—people are your number-one value, but you also have to get things done.

> **INFJs . . .**
> **get energized by the inside world**
> **look for the possibilities**
> **decide with the heart**
> **live by a plan**

A thunderous round of applause for INFJs—
they help us see the future!

What you're known for

- looking ahead—coming up with new ideas about causes that matter to people
- following through—modeling integrity and consistency
- organizing—seeing how people can best complete tasks and enjoy the process
- being creative—providing insight and imagination, especially about what matters to those around you

Top career choices

- architect
- education consultant, teacher
- fine artist, writer
- librarian
- marketer
- psychiatrist or psychologist
- religious professional
- scientist
- social worker

College and career tips

▶ Visit more than one campus, but yes, trust your hunch on which school will be best.

▶ Be sure that you make the most of classroom opportunities by limiting the number of independent studies you arrange.

▶ Find a favorite quiet study space on campus besides your room.

▶ Add a touch of realism to your expectations—double major to increase employability, compromise to meet professor expectations, etc.

Where you learn best

▶ when teachers act as mentors or take a personal interest in you

▶ if reading and writing are involved

▶ by going beyond the requirements, researching beyond the facts to the possibilities

▶ in conceptual rather than practical classes

Where you'd prefer to work or serve

▶ through words, oral or written, to impact ideas and help things change for the better

▶ leading small groups or teaching—so others can grow and develop

▶ where you can be creative—do something original, think outside the box

▶ with people who are cooperative, organized, and focused on values

How you lead people

▶ creating mutual trust among people

▶ working for cooperation instead of demanding it

▶ inspiring others with your ideas and goals

- facilitating rather than providing top-down leadership
- seeing everyone's potential, trying to get them to do their best

Hints for getting along in life

- Let others in—share some of your insights and your thinking process along the way to gain support.
- Tell others what you can do—not everyone automatically recognizes your strengths.
- Listen to others—while you often *do* know what is best, ask yourself, "What does it mean if they *are* right?"
- Ask for help—you'll face things in life you can't solve on your own, painful as that fact is!

> **INFPs. . .**
> get energized by the inside world
> look for the possibilities
> decide with the heart
> go with the flow

A thunderous round of applause for INFPs—
they remind us what the world can be!

What you're known for

▸ being lost in thought—you focus deeply on your values and feelings

▸ being optimistic—you encourage others to work toward a perfect world

▸ drawing people together—creating a common purpose, harmony, and acceptance for all

▸ having a vision—helping others see the possibilities, persuading them to honor values

Top career choices

▸ counselor

▸ education consultant

▸ English or fine arts teacher

▸ fine artist

▸ journalist

▸ psychologist or psychiatrist

▸ religious educator

▸ social scientist

▸ writer, editor

College and career tips

- ▸ Your love of possibilities may lead you to transfer colleges and/or change majors.
- ▸ Know that you may have to study harder in college; high school may have come too easily for you to have picked up the study skills you'll need.
- ▸ A second major may be necessary to meet your need for creative writing or other artistic pursuits and career-ready skills.
- ▸ Be observant and considerate—does your roommate need you to be a bit more organized?

Where you learn best

- ▸ where creativity is rewarded and you have some leeway in how you complete assignments
- ▸ if the teacher takes a personal interest in you
- ▸ when you enjoy the subject and value what you are learning
- ▸ through the arts—creative writing, music, art, theater

Where you'd prefer to work or serve

- ▸ where there is calm, quiet, cooperation, and flexibility
- ▸ through your artistic skills—music, dance, art, writing, decorating, crafts, etc.
- ▸ one-on-one, through prayer, counseling, or coaching
- ▸ close to home so you can be spontaneous, anytime you're inspired to help

How you lead people

- ▸ providing a vision, inspiring others to do right
- ▸ holding people and organizations accountable to their mission
- ▸ helping everyone reach their full potential, encouraging them to act on their ideals

- facilitating rather than dictating, creating a unique approach to leadership
- offering praise instead of criticism

Hints for getting along in life

- Tell it like it is—sometimes you have messages or criticisms others need to hear.
- Watch your idealism—it can sometimes benefit from a dose of reality.
- Reconsider the stances you take—perhaps another person's position is better for his or her situation.
- Let go of perfection—some jobs, and assignments, are *not* worth doing well.

ENFP

A thunderous round of applause
for ENFPs—they inspire us!

What you're known for

- valuing everyone—you're interested in all kinds of people and activities
- sharing resources—you know everyone and how to get information on everything
- adding vision and zest—you energize others to start new projects, champion new causes
- being warm and appreciative—you can't help making new friends

Top career choices

- artist, musician, actor
- consultant
- counselor, social scientist
- dental hygienist
- journalist
- public relations
- research assistant
- religious professional
- teacher

College and career tips

▸ Know that you may sample many majors before finding one that inspires you. Get help planning your freshman coursework so your choices don't delay graduation.

▸ Group study fits your style, but evaluate how much you're really getting done.

▸ Be careful of signing up for too many campus opportunities. Trying to do it all leads to burnout.

▸ If you're used to last-minute assignment completion, be wary. The time pressures of college may push you toward completing only things you're passionate about.

Where you learn best

▸ when there's variety—you can observe, listen, read, and interact about a subject

▸ in settings where there is room for imagination, not just facts

▸ by brainstorming, discussing ideas with peers, pondering theoretical "what-ifs"

▸ where the emphasis is on broad learning, not deadlines

Where you'd prefer to work or serve

▸ with imaginative, cooperative people who care about others

▸ missions or service-related projects where you can build relationships

▸ public speaking, evangelism, promoting what you believe in so others join the cause

▸ where you have variety, challenge, and freedom to be yourself

How you lead people

▸ using your charm and charisma to get others started

▸ motivating and encouraging everyone to be all they can be

▸ doing your best to include everyone

- ▸ providing original, ingenious ideas
- ▸ starting new efforts, then moving on to the next

Hints for getting along in life

- ▸ Find your limits—learn to manage your time and take care of yourself, recognizing fatigue and stress signs.
- ▸ Narrow your options—work with someone who is good at making decisions and master skills for bringing closure.
- ▸ Face the facts—stay alert to the things you can't change in a situation. Sometimes reality demands respect.
- ▸ Be wary of new fads—not every new idea or leader is worthy of your enthusiasm. Use your values to weigh their promises.

ENFJ

ENFJs . . .
get energized by the outside world
look for the possibilities
decide with the heart
live by a plan

A thunderous round of applause for ENFJs—
they see all that you can be!

What you're known for

► leading—you naturally start organizing so that things get done
► encouraging—you support others and help them become all they can be
► calling for integrity—monitoring values, inviting others to live up to their ideals
► seeing what could be—how organizations should treat people, believing in the positive nature of people

Top career choices

► actor, musician, artist
► consultant
► counselor or therapist
► designer
► dental assistant
► optometrist
► religious professional
► teacher
► writer

Finding the Places You Fit

College and career tips

- ▶ You may be happiest at a college with a strong emphasis on social responsibility.
- ▶ You may naturally choose a trade or major early on; check out two or three options before locking in.
- ▶ Study groups are a great option for you; step up and use your organizational skills to get the most out of the group.
- ▶ Make sure you're taking care of yourself as you engage in service activities and support your friends.

Where you learn best

- ▶ when subjects are people-oriented, discussing the needs, yearnings, and destiny of humankind
- ▶ if hard work results in personal recognition from your teachers
- ▶ if you can discuss what you're learning and interact with friends
- ▶ from warmhearted teachers who clearly communicate rules and rewards

Where you'd prefer to work or serve

- ▶ with people-oriented activities or ministries that produce results
- ▶ up front—teaching, leading, persuading, encouraging others
- ▶ creating atmospheres that include people, organizing fellowship activities that help people get along and have fun
- ▶ promoting change so that ministries or activities meet the large-scale needs of people

How you lead people

- ▶ participating as you manage people and projects
- ▶ challenging people and organizations to keep their actions in line with their values

- modeling exemplary behavior
- inspiring others to seek change
- being responsive to the needs of individuals even in large-scale efforts

Hints for getting along in life

- Don't take things personally—ask, "How would a sensible, impartial person use this criticism?"
- Get down to business—watch your emphasis on relationship, since some people just want to get the task done.
- Monitor your bossiness—you can be persuasive with your *should*s and *ought*s, but when overdone your stand may cost you more than it's worth.
- Accept less-than-perfect outcomes—cooperation can fail if others aren't playing by your rules, no matter how hard you try.

> **INTJs . . .**
> get energized by the inside world
> look for the possibilities
> decide with the head
> live by a plan

A thunderous round of applause for INTJs—
they help us envision a better way!

What you're known for

► being independent—reaching your own conclusions, being sure of their worth

► seeing what will be—generating possibilities and your own vision of the future

► changing the system—organizing, planning, working alone to meet your long-term goals

► valuing intellect and individualism—setting your own standards for achievement, confident in your belief system

Top career choices

► architect
► attorney or judge
► computer professional
► electrical or chemical engineer
► management consultant
► manager
► scientist or researcher
► electrician
► university instructor

College and career tips

▸ Excellent academics are key to finding a college fit. Lectures and debates fit your style.

▸ Narrow down the number of subjects in which you strive for expertise so that you have some time for play—drama, music, individual sports, etc.

▸ Take time to cultivate one or two friendships with like-minded students—relationships are as important to the brain as study.

▸ Give instructors a second chance to prove their competency; don't write them off too quickly.

Where you learn best

▸ in settings where you're allowed to take your own approach and choose what you'll study

▸ from teachers who challenge you and ask for extra effort

▸ through open-ended assignments, not rote learning

▸ when subjects are theoretical, systems-oriented

Where you'd prefer to work or serve

▸ with smart, effective people who take a long-term view when solving problems

▸ as teacher or coach, especially for those who value learning

▸ planning efforts, finding new approaches to traditional activities or ministries

▸ where you can work independently, creatively, and accomplish your goals

How you lead people

▸ dreaming up, designing, and building new ways of thinking and doing

▸ reorganizing the whole system if necessary

▸ being a force for change by the power of your ideas

- challenging yourself and others to work toward goals
- making decisions efficiently, seeing patterns and systems that will solve complex problems

Hints for getting along in life

- Share your ideas—bring others into your thinking before you work it all out so you can gain their commitment.
- Listen to others—write down their ideas and consider their merit instead of just tossing them out.
- Be patient—not everyone can grasp concepts as quickly as you can. Rethink how you might present information so people can catch on.
- Let others help—you'll have time to do more of the things you *really* want to do.

> INTPs . . .
> get energized by the inside world
> look for the possibilities
> decide with the head
> go with the flow

A thunderous round of applause for INTPs—
they help us define what is true!

What you're known for

- thinking—coming up with logical systems and frameworks to understand issues
- finding the truth—asking why and pointing out flaws, applying critical analysis to problems
- being independent—perhaps preferring your own thoughts to the company of others
- mastering the complex—enjoying theories, systems, and models, developing your own to explain the truth

Top career choices

- artist
- computer professional
- lawyer
- photographer
- psychologist
- respiratory therapist
- scientist or researcher
- surveyor
- writer

College and career tips

- Narrowing down schools and courses of study may be difficult. Establish your logical criteria and remember that you can transfer or change majors.
- Consider the one-course-at-a-time institutions and others where you can go steep and deep in a subject.
- Participate in at least two campus activities—sports, music, department social activities. Physical activity and socializing lead to better intellectual capacity.
- Watch your study time. You don't have to read everything ever written about a subject to complete an assignment.

Where you learn best

- when you're respected for "finding the flaws" in the thinking of others
- from competent teachers who treat you as an equal, allow you to challenge them
- through independent study, specializing in what interests you
- in scientific-oriented subjects

Where you'd prefer to work or serve

- working to solve complex problems
- researching, defining, and developing a ministry or outreach—discovering, say, the three keys to attracting other teens to volunteer
- where you can have independence, flexibility, and privacy
- reviewing past programs, classes, outreaches, events, etc., to determine what worked and what didn't

How you lead people

- influencing through theoretical ideas and your ability to analyze problems

- making decisions from a sound, logical foundation
- winning respect through your expertise, preferring to work with other experts
- interacting at an intellectual rather than personal level
- preferring that everyone work independently, systematically, so that efforts add up to the whole

Hints for getting along in life

- Avoid being an intellectual snob—other people excel at emotional, interpersonal, and intrapersonal intelligence.
- Think before you speak—not everyone can handle being critiqued or hearing why their logic is flawed.
- Warm up and lighten up—you may come across as uncaring. Remember, most work in life involves others.
- Take people breaks—purposely join committees or sports teams to get out of your head and into reality.

ENTP

A thunderous round of applause for ENTPs—
they lead us into the unknown!

What you're known for

► being confident—overcoming challenges where others see only barriers

► starting things—leading new projects, ideas, efforts with enthusiasm

► developing strategies—solving problems through insight and imagination

► taking risks—enjoying life on the edge

Top career choices

► actor

► chemical engineer

► construction worker

► computer professional

► journalist

► marketing professional

► photographer

► psychiatrist

► public relations professional

College and career tips

► Choose a college that leaves your options open, for example, offers strong drama and engineering programs.

► Seek counseling on course choices to increase your chances of graduating on time even if you change majors.

► Be wary of participating in too many activities; set priorities and pay attention to your needs for sleep, exercise, etc., to avoid burnout.

► When conceptualizing projects, watch biting off more than you can chew.

Where you learn best

► by studying concepts, not facts

► when subjects are interesting, spurring you on to dig deeper

► from teachers who allow you to challenge their positions, match wits

► if you have an audience—through speeches, debate, or peers who admire your opinions and theories

Where you'd prefer to work or serve

► on unusual projects or outreaches

► where things are changing, helping to develop strategies and solve complex problems

► flexible, challenging, unbureaucratic efforts

► up front or at the front—marketing and promoting spiritual efforts, on the mission field, or on global efforts like solving hunger

How you lead people

► challenging and encouraging people to excel

► persuading others, speaking out for change

- accepting the risk for new ideas and approaches, planning systems to meet needs
- encouraging independence in others
- envisioning what could be and modeling how to get there

Hints for getting along in life

- Cooperate—you thrive on competition, but understand how your success depends on the efforts of others.
- Be straightforward—state reality without resorting to confusing systems and models.
- Follow the rules occasionally—do the right thing instead of taking advantage of loopholes or going around someone.
- Know your limits—let go of something before chasing new opportunities. Take time to rest!

> **ENTJs . . .**
> get energized by the outside world
> look for the possibilities
> decide with the head
> live by a plan

A thunderous round of applause for ENTJs—
they bring people and plans together!

What you're known for

- leading—through structures and strategies that meet goals
- planning—thinking long-term, setting goals, and providing the energy to meet them
- solving problems—analyzing the possibilities and envisioning efficient solutions, whether it's your problem or someone else's
- understanding—developing intellectual insights about systems and organizations

Top career choices

- franchise owner
- attorney
- consultant
- human resources professional
- manager, corporate executive
- marketing or sales professional
- mortgage banker
- social services worker
- systems analyst

Finding the Places You Fit

College and career tips

▶ Early decision fits your style, but check out a few more options than feels natural.

▶ Schedules and goals for study suit you well; look for like-minded students if you organize a study group.

▶ With your competitive drive and desire to achieve, watch for early signs of stress—irritability, being overly critical, changes in sleep pattern, etc.

▶ Schedule time to play!

Where you learn best

▶ in subjects you know will help you "get ahead"

▶ by critiquing and solving problems

▶ from well-organized, challenging teachers

▶ through critical feedback, which you view as opportunities for learning

Where you'd prefer to work or serve

▶ leading, planning, developing

▶ fundraising and other areas that deal with finances

▶ with efficient, goal-oriented, tough-minded people who want to be challenged

▶ working to change structures to make the world a better place

How you lead people

▶ managing directly, being tough when necessary

▶ taking charge when a strong leader is needed

▶ developing a model, then using it to guide actions and long-range vision

▶ modeling dedication, confidence, concentration

▶ standing firm on principles, against opposition

Hints for getting along in life

- ▸ Set aside your goals—practice being in the moment and just enjoy an adventure.
- ▸ Let someone else lead occasionally—develop their potential and let them share in running the world!
- ▸ Find a personal critic—run your ideas past someone who will keep you from being overly confident.
- ▸ Be patient—systems and organizations can't change as fast as you can envision solutions!

7

How Not to Spin
in Your Socks

Back in the early 1980s, Gregor Dimitriov defected from the
dictator-controlled Soviet Union for freedom in the United
States. Yet after six months in America, he voluntarily returned to the country he had fled, knowing he'd be jailed by the
communist government. Gregor received a four-year prison sen-
tence. Asked why he returned, he simply said, "I couldn't decide."

Gregor was overwhelmed by *choices*. In the Soviet Union he had
stood in line at stores that each sold one staple—bread, milk, meat.
In American supermarkets, Gregor spun in the aisles. He was overwhelmed by options. When he needed to go somewhere, no one
told him whether he should take a bus—or a car, train, or bike. Once
he knew he needed a car, no one dictated it should be a Honda—or
a Toyota, Nissan, Chevy, or Ford.

Your own choices may have you spinning in your socks.

The odds aren't good that your life will slow down. There's no
way to screw your feet to the floor to keep stable. And you don't
have a guaranteed bowl of rice and a bed of lice waiting for you in

a Soviet *gulag*. You have to make matter-of-fact, day-to-day choices just to survive. Even more than that, to thrive.

In case you haven't noticed, life keeps spinning faster. Remember when summer seemed to last forever? You were almost *glad* to get back to school. Unless you decide to be a permanent student or to become a teacher, your summer freedom will eventually come to a halt. Once you step into the world of work, your only taste of summer may be in your daydreams.

Life: Full Speed Ahead

The speed of life isn't the only issue. The *demands* of life step up as well.

Flash forward fifteen or twenty years. Every decision you make feels big. You've got cars to wash and career cliffs to climb. A significant someone and maybe a brood of children. That means in-laws. Phones buzz, emails overflow your inbox, everyone expects you to meet their demands first. More bills, more responsibilities, more choices. Putting Grandma's house painting on your calendar doesn't help if you say yes to too many other requests.

So . . . how will you fit it all in?

Some people believe that if you handle things right, you'll have time for everything.

You won't.

You have to make choices.

You'll never fit the important things into life unless you make room for them *first*. Even finding your fit won't do you any good if you don't make time in your schedule to apply what you know.

We aren't going to ram you through a crash course in time management. But we'd like to share five key Bible truths about time that might make it easier to put the ideas of *Find Your Fit* to work in your life.

From the start of his formal ministry to his death, Jesus had only three years to change the world. Yet Jesus managed to start the church. Develop deep friendships. Go fishing. Attend feasts and parties. Tell stories. Laugh with children. Have a leisurely meal with people whose company he enjoyed. How did he do it?

Time Truth #1: Jesus put his relationship with God first

Jesus shocked his hearers when he addressed God as "Daddy" (see Mark 14:36, for example). Even if right now your life at home isn't perfect, picture the mommies and daddies of your childhood dreams. They're the people we like to be with. They toss us in the air, bounce us on their knees, give us pennies to toss in fountains. Jesus consistently fought for time alone with his Father despite crowds who pushed to be near him, masses who sought healing, and close friends and disciples who badly needed training. Jesus still found time for his relationship with God.

If God is truly going to be the center of your life, you have to carve out time to spend on your relationship.

God won't push. You've already been invited to spend time with God, so the response belongs to you.

We're not talking—necessarily—about hauling out of bed hours before the rest of the world is awake. Just as people differ in what they like to do with friends on Saturday nights—good stuff, we mean—people differ in what adds up to meaningful, growing time with God. If the thought of knocking off a chapter of the Bible and an hour of prayer every morning makes you want to yank the covers over your head, you have lots of company—even among the strongest of Christians.

We could write several more books on ideas to make your time with God as good as time with your best friend—especially since you'll find out they're one and the same. But do this: Keep plugging until you find a group of Jesus followers and some helpful habits to keep you close to God.

Why? When you stay close to God you get *constant love*. You're loved for who you are—not whether you have a date for prom, not because you're perfect. You get *direction*. Living for God isn't about rules you have to do if you want to be righteous. Jesus remakes us from the inside out.

Jesus called himself the bread of life (John 6:35). Time with God is the only nourishment that allows you to be who you were meant to be *and* have the resources to act for God.

Time Truth #2: Jesus knew his mission

Jesus knew that his goal on earth was to plant the seeds of the kingdom of God. That goal helped him focus on what he needed to do—moving from place to place, reaching as many people as he could, equipping followers and sending them out by themselves to practice spreading the good news.

Sometimes Jesus' choices were tough. He had to leave towns when people clamored to be healed or to seek his wisdom. He had to come down from the mountains and God's presence to be with people clueless about him or his message. And lots of other people wanted to define Jesus' mission for him:

- ► Israelites who detested the Romans wanted him to set himself up as king.
- ► Many in the crowds who followed him wanted food and health.
- ► Judas thought he should erase poverty.
- ► The scribes and Pharisees wanted him to enforce the laws of Moses—and all the quibbles and bits added to it over the centuries.

It isn't too soon to start thinking about your own mission in life. As you've worked through *Find Your Fit*, maybe you've caught glimpses of what God wants you to be.

You can trust that God's plans are good. You can open your heart to what God wants. No matter how dangerous it may seem to trust

God with your life, it's infinitely more dangerous to live your life outside of God's will. It's your choice, however, because God doesn't use puppets. You can include or exclude God as you design your mission for life.

You can also trust that God's view of you is true. God is working in you. God has a plan, and you're part of it. You can make a difference if you understand what God wants you to do.

God's view of you says you can be different and you can make a difference. Plenty of teens have already discovered that and can say how they want to change their corner of the world.

- From a girl who counsels teens with life-threatening illnesses: "I got so much support when I was ill that I want to give back to the hospital and community."

- From a boy who tutors younger children: "I can show them that smart teens are cool and get them started on that path."

- From a student who is a junior counselor in city recreational programs: "I've got time. I can use it to make a difference or to get into trouble."

- From a boy who works with the Red Cross and coordinated construction of a neighborhood hockey rink: "I'm responsible to help out."

- From a girl who tutors immigrant adults for their citizenship examinations: "I want others to have the confidence and opportunities I have."

- From a teen who championed a day-care center at her high school for teen mothers: "I can't help helping people when the cards are stacked against them."*

These teens know their actions matter, and the smiles on the faces of people they help signal a heap of good things are going on. They're beginning to understand their missions, and it's shaping

*"Meet 10 Teen Heroes," *Minneapolis Star Tribune*, April 23, 1998, E2.

their plans to be teachers, lawyers, pediatricians. The specifics of their plans will change, but their goal of making a difference won't.

Time Truth #3: Jesus kept his life in balance

If you sign up for God's plan, that doesn't mean you spend every spare moment being sucked dry by the needs of others. You get to enjoy God's creation, fun times with friends, learning for the joy of it, the ups and downs of families. In other words, you get a balanced life.

Jesus modeled that life for you. When he was tired, he rested. When the crowds overwhelmed him, he left. When he received bad news, he retreated with his best friends. If Jesus had time for weddings, boat rides, visits with close friends, and his relationship with God, then so do you.

And you have to be filled up to serve. Ditch the image of servants of God who wear themselves out, neglect their families, and die of exhaustion. Jesus said he came not just so you'd have life, but abundant life—a life with plenty of resources, incredible richness (John 10:10). Not riches, but richness. You can't concentrate on the needs of others if you're always maxed out. You don't want to feel like someone else is driving your car in the race of life—and you're just along as a passenger, ready to lean out the window and heave when the car hits the curves.

So how do you create a balanced life? Accept that you're a multifaceted person. God expects you to take care of yourself.

- ► You've got a *brain* to feed. Sure, learning gives you something to talk about besides the latest Oscar winners. (Don't say, "I'm not that good at school." Did you know that there's a link between Alzheimer's and people who stop using their brains?)
- ► You've got a *spirit* to nourish. God wants to pour love, joy, peace, patience, kindness, goodness, faithfulness, gentleness, and self-control into your life. (Don't say, "I'm not into spiritual growth." God wants to give you inward strength.)

► You've got a *body* to tend. Not just avoiding hurting your body with immoral sex or illegal drugs, but making exercise an immovable rock in your schedule. Find moves you like to do and do them. (Don't say, "I'm not a jock." After all, by the time you reach full adulthood, you can be in far better shape than the heroes of high school football.)

Look at the word *recreation* carefully. *Re*-creation. Balancing your life puts you on the path to being all you can be, allowing yourself to be zapped with God's creative powers.

Time Truth #4: Jesus kept it simple

Have you ever seen a movie or even a picture where Jesus or his disciples carried *anything*? They must have hauled a couple of tent rolls as they traveled. Maybe packed a kettle and a spork for cooking. What about a change of clothes? Surely they must have brought along a few things, but one reason Jesus was so available to others was that he kept his life simple. He meant it when he said,

> Consider the lilies of the field, how they grow; they neither toil nor spin, yet I tell you, even Solomon in all his glory was not clothed like one of these. But if God so clothes the grass of the field, which is alive today and tomorrow is thrown into the oven, will [God] not much more clothe you—you of little faith?
>
> Matthew 6:28–30 NRSV

The Bible does show people of wealth, including Joseph of Arimathea (who provided the tomb where Jesus was buried) and Lydia (whose home the early Christians used as a gathering place). It isn't money, but the *love* of money that's the root of all evil.

But—things complicate our lives. We own things. They also own us.

Do you have a car? You pay a price for the freedom wheels give you. Like earning the money for insurance and gas. Time out for oil changes and engine maintenance. Hours at the license bureau. From beginning to end, you have to figure out what to buy, then maintain it, repair it, and dispose of it when it breaks.

That's why lifestyle choices are so important—how much stuff you have determines how much time you have available.

Decide now to have doable dreams. Jane and Kevin both raised their families in decent homes in the burbs, but each family managed to have one parent stay home with preschoolers. How? From the get-go they decided against huge mortgages and car payments that required a second income.

A simple lifestyle isn't like taking vows to be a monk. It's weighing the benefits you get against the time and freedom you give up.

Time Truth #5: Jesus knew what it meant to shine

Jesus told us, "You are the light of the world. A city built on a hill cannot be hid. . . . Let your light shine before others, so that they may see your good works and give glory to your Father in heaven" (Matthew 5:14, 16 NRSV). Two thousand years later, Andy Warhol said, "In the future, everyone will be world famous for fifteen minutes."

There's more than one way to shine famously. You can do something incredibly stupid, astoundingly evil, extraordinarily lucky, disastrously unfortunate—or astonishingly well.

Some people have two fifteen-minute moments of fame. First they shine, then they fall. The athletes convicted of domestic abuse. The televangelists jailed for tax evasion. The politicians shielding their faces from news cameras after charges of sexual harassment and worse. And some fall, only to return to shine. The ex-addicts who use all their resources for a drop-in counseling center. The former female inmate who works to establish an education program for convicts that are mothers of young children.

It all makes fame sound pretty dangerous. But there's another kind of fame, one that's seldom on the evening news. It's subtle— even invisible. It's doing what you were meant to do, right where God wants you to do it, no matter what anyone else thinks. It's living out the words of Paul:

> Do everything without grumbling or arguing, so that you may become blameless and pure, "children of God without fault in a crooked and depraved generation." Then you will shine among them like stars in the sky as you hold firmly to the word of life.
>
> Philippians 2:14–16

Think of people you admire. Not the ones in their fifteen minutes of fame, but the folks who shine for God. Do you wonder how they arrange their lives so they can shine for God?

Guess what? You have just as much time to shine for God as they do—as many minutes in each hour, as many hours in each day. Over a lifetime the people who shine are those who recognize God's call and arrange their lives to answer.

You can be a person who shines. Answering God's call might put you in medical school, on a board of directors, in front of a classroom of children, at a homeless shelter—wherever God wants you to be.

You'll have goals and a purpose.

You'll know why you do what you do.

You'll define for yourself what success means and you'll have your eyes on that prize—not what the world says you need.

You'll understand there's trouble in this world. If it comes your way, you'll realize that's just life, not God's anger. And you'll know God is with you no matter what.

You'll have located your spot in the plans of the God who is able to "keep you from stumbling and to present you before his glorious presence without fault and with great joy" (Jude 24).

You'll have found your fit.

Why Doesn't God Just Hand You the Directions?

Are you wondering if finding your fit is too confusing? Worried that you might forever ruin your life if you come up with the "wrong" answer? Wishing life weren't so complicated or that God—or your parents or school—would just type up directions for you and put them on the back of a cereal box?

Imagine if God really did tell you exactly what to do—showing up in a burning bush that shouts, "Apply to Harvaaaard. Major in cake decoratinnnng. Buy sixteen shares of Amazon-dot-commmmm. . . ." And off you'd go.

Then imagine, too, how you would feel. You're *told* exactly what to do. (Isn't that exactly what you like best about being a teenager—people telling you what to do?) And we're guessing that one day you'd wake up and feel like you missed something. You would realize that uncertainty and failure aren't the worst things in life. In fact, "confusion" and "problems" are actually some of life's biggest blessings.

Think of everything you experience because God *doesn't* simply drop a life plan on you:

You get to explore

The adventure of discovery is a highlight of being human. You might not trek to the other side of the globe, but you can explore *you* and how you fit in an ever-widening world all around you. It's a frontier no one else can explore. Yes, we can give you quizzes and people can tell you what they observe, but only you can put all of the pieces together—after all, only you have any experience being you.

And does it really matter that you miss some moves while you're checking out who you are? The whole point of exploring is to bump into stuff you don't even know is there! Accidental detours are sometimes fantastic exploits full of crazy friendships and priceless discoveries—even if you just find out what it takes to do another person's job.

You get to choose

We're wired to want to make our own choices—it's the free-will thing God built into us and our world. Parents know that if you really want a two-year-old to put on shoes, you say, "Would you like to wear your tennis shoes or sandals?" so they think they have a choice. Not, "Put on your shoes right now!" (at least not the first time). And even as adults, people want a say in what happens to them.

Many of the adults who take *LifeKeys*, the course *Find Your Fit* is based on, tell us things like these:

- ► "My parents said they wouldn't pay for college unless I became a doctor."
- ► "I had no choice but to take over the family business."
- ► "I didn't choose a career—everyone said I'd just marry and have babies anyway."

Sometimes as these people re-choose a career through *LifeKeys*, they discover that the path they were pushed down actually does suit them. Sometimes they opt for change. But by making their own choices—finding their fit based on God, not others—they buy into their future.

You get to struggle

Maybe it would sound like a relief to only take classes you're good at. But be honest—haven't you had a tough class turn out great because of a zany teacher? Or where you bonded with a new friend over brutal homework? Or when you finally earned a good grade because of hair-pulling, late-evening, determined hard work—and you felt like a genius? Some of life's best things come only through struggle.

You get to choose your friends

Sure, sometimes you wish your whole crew wanted to see the same movie, but disagreements and discussions and opinions are what life is all about. Not to mention that with a variety of friends, you get to try rock climbing or impressionist painting or making sushi just because someone else knows all about it.

You get to fail

What's so great about failure? Provided no one's laughing at you, it's a God-given chance to grow patience and self-control. And failing when you're young is the best preparation for being an adult who can say things like, "I made a mistake. I'm sorry." Besides, when you learn it's okay to fail at little things—like finding out you're better at clarinet than drums—it cuts the dread out of trying new things. And you learn that no one's good at everything.

You get to decide who you are

You gain firsthand proof that God designed you for a great, unique, fulfilling life. And you find out that God keeps promises. You have a future!

If you're trying to do what God has in mind, even detours can turn out to be just what you need to make the most of your future. Jane started out as a bank examiner—*not* a good fit for her personality type (INFJ). But she met great people, learned about business, completed an MBA, did lots of writing, and meandered to being a controller, a consultant, and finally a writer—on subjects as far removed from finance as possible. Jane's journey wasn't a straight line from A to B, but as she looks back, each detour gave her valuable experiences and wisdom.

By the time he was in high school, Kevin knew he wanted to be in full-time service, but he didn't know where. He flip-flopped through a variety of majors—from plant science to Mandarin Chinese to teaching—until he landed in courses heavy in writing. As he trained in graduate school, he discovered he liked working with youth and was able to pastor a large youth group for more than five years. He couldn't have planned on a couple decades of writing and editing because it's a rare way to make a living. But he's continued to write as he's learned to coach people though career changes. Who knew that role would tie together everything he's done with his life so far?

Karen was fascinated by history and social issues in high school and finished a political science major with great grades, but after trying some political work, she realized she wasn't fulfilled. Some research helped her realize she valued helping people directly, so she tried another form of social science and got a master's degree in counseling. Now, looking back, she can see that what has really fascinated her all along is people, and especially what motivates them.

We're not shocked that each of us has had multiple dreams and a sequence of careers. Some adults go through seven *careers*, not seven jobs. You might have even more. But we aren't hung up about our futures. Why?

We've found our fit.

We know what we do well.

We've got a handle on our values.

We've practiced choosing between right and right in the world of work and are still on course.

And most important, we've got real-world proof of what we share in this book. We can look back and see how God guided all our planning and decision-making and shot-in-the-dark choices and even misguided choices. We know we can trust God.

Now it's *your* chance to get started on the path that will build your trust in God. It's the path that fits you best. But there isn't just one right fit. You may find two or three in your lifetime.

And you won't figure out your fit in just a quick flip through this book. It may take weeks, months, or even years, depending on where you started—because in order to *Find Your Fit*, you have to be able to say some things like you mean it:

▸ "I'm made in God's image." Can you say that? And believe what it implies—that you are valuable just as you are because God created you uniquely?

- "God gave me a special blend of life gifts, spiritual gifts, personality type, and values. I'm fearfully and wonderfully made." Are you convinced that God gave you just the right gifts for who you are?
- "God has plans for me, to flourish and do good works." Are you going to keep searching out how God wants you to passionately use your talents and gifts?

However you fit into God's plan, rest assured it's a *perfect* fit. Not a hand-me-down slot, but a place where you can

do what you do best

revel in being part of something huger than yourself

know God

be different

and make a difference

So How Do You Plan a Life?

Now that you've worked through this book, where do you go from here?

Take a look at these suggestions and make a plan. Don't let your career—or your whole life, really—just happen to you. Start exploring the possibilities.

1. Find a *Find Your Fit* partner

Finding your fit is a big job. You can do some of it yourself, but the best decisions and insights involve getting ideas and feedback from others. Consider partnering with these folks:

- **Your parents.** Make sure they read over your results and know what you've been thinking about. They've already been through the types of decisions you're making right now, and they've already got a lot invested in your future.

- **Your friends.** They're in the same boat and on a similar timeline. Share your results with your friends or classmates. Maybe you could start a *Find Your Fit* small group or keep talking about your ideas and discoveries.
- **Adult mentors.** Lots of adults are willing to lend a hand to teens who want to figure themselves out or make plans for the future. Ask your parents who they know, talk to your teachers or leaders, or think of others in your life who might be willing to talk with you about their jobs.

2. Record your thoughts

Keep writing down ideas or observations as they come to you: career ideas, why majors or careers do/don't appeal to you, schools or majors you might want to follow up on, factors that fit your personality. Be willing to dream and write it all down.

3. Use your classes strategically

Take classes in subject areas you're curious about. Scope out the subject matter as well as the people who do well in the class and seem to enjoy it. How well do you fit with them? Could you see yourself wanting to take more classes in that subject? Consider taking classes through community colleges, too.

4. Volunteer or get some experience

If you have any choice about part-time work, go for a job that could get you closer to an area of your interest, not just make you money. If you're into cars, go work for a car dealership. If you like the idea of medicine, you can volunteer at a hospital. Think creatively and make your jobs count.

5. Visit your school counselor or career services office

He or she can provide you with a lot of resources that they've gathered up to help students transition from high school to their next step in life. Websites, handouts, connections with colleges, etc., are all worth checking out. Sometimes college representatives come to visit high schools—go listen! Or go to a career or college fair to explore your options.

6. Check out the timeline at the end of the book

It gives you concrete steps to finding your fit at each stage over the next several years.

**Keep looking and thinking,
and you WILL find your fit!**

Keep Finding Your Fit

Five Things to Do Every Year in High School and College for College and Career Success

Now that you've spent all this time learning about yourself and the way God made you, let's get practical! You can start implementing your new insights by reading through the steps below and taking action. There are five suggested action steps for each year of high school and college, so everyone can find something appropriate for your situation. Be bold and try something new! It will pay off.

Ninth Grade

1. Learn how to learn in high school! Mastering a higher level of responsibility and more homework may take some time, but it's worth it. A low GPA from early high school takes a lot of hard work to overcome later.

2. Spend some time talking with your parents about all of the class choices your high school offers. Parents, help your child

understand what the courses are like, and have a good conversation about what to take when.

3. Visit your high school guidance counselor or dean and have a good conversation about classes and other options your high school offers. Parents, make use of teacher conferences to get a clear understanding of how your student is doing, and talk with your teen about what you hear.

4. Join something! Get involved in your high school and try at least a couple of things—music, sports, clubs, anything. Nothing helps a student understand what they like better than trying things outside of class.

5. Find ways to get involved outside of school as well, to get a broader perspective of the world outside of the school environment. Volunteering, youth group, scouting, babysitting, or a first job are relatively easy ways to get involved and maybe find an interest you wouldn't otherwise find.

Tenth Grade

1. This is usually the first year when students take AP and other honors courses. Think of them as experiments—every class is a chance to see whether you've found the appropriate level of challenge in that subject. Then adjust accordingly. You don't have to excel at everything equally.

2. Keep trying new activities at school. You don't have to keep doing something just because you did it last year. It takes courage to try new groups and meet new people, but it can be worth it!

3. Start looking for summer activities, classes, or camps that might match up with your interest areas. Pay attention to announcements at school and talk with your parents about your ideas. Parents, look for opportunities like one- or two-week programs in science, coding, theater, or writing.

4. Look for a college fair to attend or start doing some quick college visits with your family or friends. Sometimes high school groups or teams will go to college campuses. Take advantage of chances like these to look around and start getting an idea of what various colleges are like.

5. Watch for opportunities to take the PSAT (usually in the spring) or practice ACT or SAT tests. It's good for you to get your eyes on these tests early so you know what to expect next year. The PSAT opens the door to be considered for National Merit Scholarships, so it's worth trying.

Eleventh Grade

1. Junior year is usually when classes take a step up in difficulty. It's also the year when you set the GPA that colleges will see on your transcript when you apply, so take your classes seriously. Keep adjusting your study strategies if needed and choose classes for senior year strategically.

2. Look for ways to take a career interest test or personality inventory at school or with a career or college counselor. These tests are a great follow-up step after completing *Find Your Fit*, and the conversations you have about the results can really help you set goals for a career or major.

3. This is the year to do as much college visiting as you can. Think of it like window-shopping—you're looking around to figure out what you like and what you don't. Educate yourself by doing some of your own college research so you can figure out what you want to look for.

4. Step into leadership positions with groups or teams you're part of. You don't need to lead everything, but having at least one leadership position on your college applications demonstrates initiative. Leadership at work or in summer camps, volunteering, etc., all count!

5. Map out a strategy for taking entrance exams like the PSAT, SAT, and ACT. Keep track of registration deadlines and plan to take the ACT/SAT two or three times to get your score as high as you can. Finish up your test-taking before your senior year so you know which colleges you'll be able to get into.

Twelfth Grade

1. Your first task is to create a final list of colleges to apply to. Sit down with your parents and go over your visits, check the ACT/SAT averages, and look at the academic and extracurricular opportunities that each college offers. Judge each school by the overall fit and its affordability.

2. Take on your classes and don't slack off. Colleges will see your transcript! Use senior year to prepare for the difficulty of college classes. If you can, take classes that can get you college credit—either at your high school or a local college. That experience will help you get ready.

3. Plan to get your college applications done by October 31 so that you can meet any early deadlines. If you start in August or September, it's very doable. Ask for letters of recommendation early and allow time for your test scores to be sent. Draft essays and get them reviewed before you send.

4. Parents, make sure you file the FAFSA and other financial aid application paper work as soon as you can. Financial aid deadlines are usually separate from application deadlines, but you want to finish both by Thanksgiving, if possible. Research the FAFSA process carefully to avoid mistakes.

5. Plan to do a second round of college visits once you know where you're admitted, in winter or early spring. Those final visits are crucial to get the last pieces of information you need in order to make your decision by May 1. Talk to professors and students to get inside perspectives.

College Freshman

1. Think like a ninth-grader—you're a freshman all over again, so you have some of the same challenges. Learning how to learn and succeed at the college level is a challenge for a lot of new college students. Make sure you start building study skills that will get you off to a good start.

2. Be a joiner! You'll want to join at least one group, club, or sport that will help you meet people and keep you busy. Student organizations are a much bigger deal at the college level. They raise money, travel abroad, and throw big events. There's usually at least one for every major. And get involved in ministry inside and outside the church—a local congregation, campus groups, and other organizations that let you join other followers of Jesus in putting all of yourself into action.

3. Even if you think you know what you want to study, use every opportunity you have to explore different interest areas and possibilities. Something you've never thought about might end up being the perfect thing for you. Your academic advisor can help you choose courses each term.

4. Look for ways to get some work experience. Even if you don't think it "counts" because it's not related to your major, it will help you fill up your résumé. Employers like hiring students with at least some experience. On-campus jobs may not be glamorous, but they're a good place to start.

5. Start paying attention to the career development office on your campus. They will be making announcements and offering events that you can participate in, like career fairs and workshops. You could take a career test, line up a job shadow, or learn about jobs related to your major.

College Sophomore

1. By the end of sophomore year, you will typically be required to choose and declare a major officially. Make sure you've

investigated your options thoroughly by reading the list of required classes, trying a course or two, and talking with a professor and student in the department.

2. If you haven't already, it's time to write a résumé. You might need it for all kinds of things—your first internship, a new job, a scholarship, or a summer research program. Don't use the templates in Word—write it yourself with help from the career development office.

3. Sophomore and junior year are the most common times to use for studying abroad or studying away (e.g., in New York, LA, or Chicago). Some programs also include an internship! If that's something you want to do, make time for it and plan ahead by talking to your academic advisor.

4. Keep your eyes open for ways to learn about career fields related to your major. Go listen to guest speakers, go to a career fair, do some research online, talk to a professor or older student. You won't know what you want to do unless you take steps to learn about your options.

5. Step up in the groups you've joined and take advantage of everything they're offering. Volunteer in the community, lead a project, make a presentation—anything that will give you new experiences or teach you new skills is worthwhile. This is an important résumé builder.

College Junior

1. Continue working through your major requirements and finalize any additional majors/minors you might want to add. As the coursework gets harder, make sure you're keeping pace. Your GPA in your major will matter the most, so keep working hard and get some help if you need it.

2. Start refining your list of activities and priorities down to things that are the most important and relevant to your life

after college. Move up into a leadership position if you can. Build a résumé that demonstrates focused attention to the skills and experiences needed for your career field.

3. Your main priority should be getting an internship this year or next summer. If you are going into a science field, a research experience might be even better. Finding and applying for these experiences can take some hard work and persistence. Your career development office can help.

4. If you're considering graduate school, start looking at universities and their programs. Make sure you understand the admission requirements. Prepare for and complete any entrance exams required, like the GRE, LSAT, MCAT, or GMAT. Most students start on exams in the spring.

5. Take advantage of every opportunity to talk with professionals in your area of interest. Networking is a skill every student needs to develop. Set up a LinkedIn account and connect with people through it. Introduce yourself to anyone who might be able to help. Connections matter!

College Senior

1. Seniors should be winding down major requirements. You may be working on a senior project or research paper. Use your final classes to sum up your learning and start relating it to real world implications. Build positive relationships with professors so they'll be references for you.

2. If you're applying to graduate school, you should be finalizing applications by December 1, and some applications are due much earlier! Personal statements are the hardest part, so get some help with writing them. Send your transcripts and exam scores, and prepare for any interviews.

3. Now is the time to get serious about getting hired. Spend some time researching companies that you could be interested in

working for. Use every opportunity to network, join a professional association, follow companies on LinkedIn, and seek out job search help from the career office.

4. Interviewing skills will become very important this year. Everyone needs practice, so look for ways to do a mock interview or an interview on campus. Ask a friend or parent to rehearse with you and give you feedback. Read over job descriptions and think of likely questions for that job.

5. Polish your résumé and continue updating it based on feedback. Develop different versions for different types of jobs. Begin sending it in paper or electronic formats. Accompany each résumé with a cover letter tailored to the job. Keep good records of application activities and follow up.

All about Me

I have identified the following interests:

My top three ability themes are _____ _____ _____ *. I know I have these abilities:*

I believe I have the following spiritual gifts:

My top eight values:

_____   _____

_____   _____

_____   _____

_____   _____

With my personality preferences for _____,
these things are important as I choose places to put my gifts to use:

Values

- ___ accuracy
- ___ achievement
- ___ advancement
- ___ adventure
- ___ aesthetics
- ___ artistic expression
- ___ authenticity
- ___ balance
- ___ challenge
- ___ competency
- ___ competition
- ___ conformity
- ___ contribution
- ___ control
- ___ cooperation
- ___ creativity
- ___ efficiency
- ___ fairness

- ___ family
- ___ financial security
- ___ flexibility
- ___ friendship
- ___ generosity
- ___ happiness
- ___ humor
- ___ independence
- ___ influence
- ___ integrity
- ___ learning
- ___ leisure
- ___ location
- ___ love
- ___ loyalty
- ___ nature
- ___ organization
- ___ peace

- ___ perseverance
- ___ personal development
- ___ physical fitness and health
- ___ power
- ___ prestige
- ___ purity
- ___ recognition
- ___ relationship with God
- ___ responsibility
- ___ security
- ___ self-respect
- ___ service
- ___ stability
- ___ tolerance
- ___ tradition
- ___ variety

Jane Kise, EdD, is an author and consultant with extensive experience in leadership, executive coaching, team building, and improving classroom instruction. She is considered a worldwide expert in Jungian personality type and its impact on both leadership and education. The author of over twenty-five books, she works with schools and businesses, facilitating the creation of environments where everyone—leaders, teachers, and students—can flourish.

A frequent keynote speaker, her past engagements include conferences across the United States and in Europe, Saudi Arabia, Australia, and New Zealand. She holds an MBA from the Carlson School of Management and a doctorate in education leadership from the University of St. Thomas. You can read more about her work at www.janekise.com.

Kevin Johnson is the bestselling author or coauthor of more than sixty books and study Bibles for youth, children, and adults. As the pastor of more than four hundred middle schoolers in a pioneering megachurch, he mobilized more than half of his students into weekly volunteering, contributing nearly a thousand hours a month inside and outside church walls.

Making the most of his background as a youthworker, nonfiction editor, teaching pastor, and solo pastor, Kevin is now a career and executive coach. He has helped hundreds of clients across numerous industries, levels, and functions take bold next steps in work and life. He holds an MDiv from Fuller Theological Seminary and a BA in English and print journalism from the University of

Wisconsin–River Falls. Learn more about Kevin at www.kevinjohnson books.com.

Karen Eilers is an experienced career and college counselor with over ten years of experience working with high schoolers, college students, and young adults on all aspects of career development and college planning. Her passion is unleashing the talents of each person she works with so that they can find their own success.

Karen has been designated a Master Career Specialist by the National Career Development Association, holds a master's degree in student development in post-secondary education from the University of Iowa, and has worked at two private colleges as a director of career development and director of internships.

Karen coaches students and young adults through her private practice, Motivated Careers, LLC, and through University Funding Professionals. She also volunteers in her church high school ministry and leads workshops for community groups on career and personal development topics. Learn more at www.motivated careers.com.

ACCURACY

Being true or correct in
attention to detail

PSALM 147:4

ACHIEVEMENT

Enjoying a sense of
accomplishment

ECCLESIASTES 2:24–25

ADVANCEMENT

Striving to gain opportunities
for growth or seniority

PROVERBS 22:29

ADVENTURE

Seeking new and exciting
challenges that may
include taking risks

GENESIS 12:1–2

AESTHETICS

Appreciating what
is beautiful

PHILIPPIANS 4:8

ARTISTIC EXPRESSION

Expressing yourself
through the arts—painting,
drama, literature, etc.

1 KINGS 6:29–32

AUTHENTICITY

Ongoing desire to honestly
express who you are

JAMES 1:22–25

BALANCE

Giving proper weight to
each area of your life

ECCLESIASTES 3:1–8

CHALLENGE

Attracted to new
problems, difficult tasks

HEBREWS 10:35–36

COMPETENCY

Wanting to meet or exceed
standards or expectations

2 CORINTHIANS 3:4–5

COMPETITION

Matching efforts or abilities
with yourself or others

1 CORINTHIANS 9:25

CONFORMITY

Preferring to be like
others, not standing out

ROMANS 12:2

CONTRIBUTION

Giving or making a
difference for others

EPHESIANS 2:10

CONTROL

Being in charge or
wanting to have influence
over outcomes

PROVERBS 25:28

COOPERATION

Striving for good
relationships and teamwork

COLOSSIANS 3:12–15

CREATIVITY

Being imaginative
and innovative, going
outside the norm

2 CHRONICLES 2:13–14

EFFICIENCY

Working to accomplish tasks
in less time than expected

PROVERBS 13:4

FAIRNESS

Ensuring that rules,
situations, opportunities
work for all

LUKE 6:38B

FAMILY

Making family
relationships important

EPHESIANS 6:2–3

FINANCIAL SECURITY

Being free from
financial worries

LUKE 12:16–20

FLEXIBILITY

Coping easily with
change and surprise

JAMES 4:13–15

FRIENDSHIP

Making close, personal
relationships important

ECCLESIASTES 4:9–10

GENEROSITY

Giving easily

2 CORINTHIANS 9:7–8

HAPPINESS

Finding satisfaction,
joy, or pleasure

PSALM 37:3–4

HUMOR

Enjoying funny stuff

PROVERBS 17:22

INDEPENDENCE

Wanting control of your
own time, behavior, tasks

GALATIANS 6:4–5

INFLUENCE

Capacity to affect or shape
people, processes, or ideas

MATTHEW 5:13–16

INTEGRITY

Making what you say and
what you do the same thing

PROVERBS 11:3

LEARNING

Wanting to grow in
understanding

PROVERBS 1:5–7

LEISURE

Appreciating unstructured
or unscheduled time

ECCLESIASTES 8:15

LOYALTY

Trying to be faithful,
constant, and steadfast

PROVERBS 18:24

LOVE

Cherishing yourself or others

1 JOHN 4:7–8

LOCATION

Preferring a specific
place, neighborhood, or
area of the country that
matches your lifestyle

PSALM 139:7–10

NATURE

Liking to be outdoors

PSALM 19:1–3

ORGANIZATION

Being in control of time,
priorities, possessions,
and/or processes

EXODUS 18:19–22

PEACE

Wanting tranquility
and serenity

PHILIPPIANS 4:6–7

PERSEVERANCE

Sticking to your
goals and ideals

JAMES 1:2–4

PERSONAL DEVELOPMENT

Wanting to use your potential
and grow to the fullest

1 TIMOTHY 4:14–15

PHYSICAL FITNESS & HEALTH

Respect for your body,
enjoying sports or fitness

1 CORINTHIANS 6:19–20

POWER

Wanting to sell, persuade,
lead, or influence others

1 PETER 5:2–4

PRESTIGE

Having or showing success,
rank, wealth, or status

MATTHEW 20:25–28

PURITY

Wanting to do the right
thing for the right reasons

MATTHEW 5:8

RECOGNITION

Desiring the respect of others
or credit for achievements

PROVERBS 22:1

RELATIONSHIP WITH GOD

Sticking close to the
God who made you

PSALM 119:35–37

RESPONSIBILITY

Being accountable
for outcomes

JOHN 15:10–11

SECURITY

Feeling safe and confident
about the future

PSALM 91:1–2

SELF-RESPECT

Having pride or a sense
of personal identity

PSALM 139:14

SERVICE

Helping others or
contributing to society

ISAIAH 58:6–8

STABILITY

Maintaining continuity,
consistency, and predictability
over a period of time

PSALM 57:7

TOLERANCE

Accepting or remaining
open to the viewpoints
and values of others

EPHESIANS 4:32

TRADITION

Treasuring customs and
links with the past

PSALM 79:13

_____

_____

_____

_____

_____

_____

_____

_____

_____

_____

_____

_____

_____

_____

_____

_____

_____

_____

_____

_____

VARIETY

Desiring new and different
activities, frequent change

GENESIS 1:31–2:1

_____

_____

_____

_____

_____

_____

_____

_____

_____

_____

_____

_____

_____

_____

_____

_____

_____

_____

_____

_____

These are
VERY VALUABLE
to me

These are
VALUABLE
to me

These are
NOT VERY VALUABLE
to me